Sons of Survivors

Making Peace with Inherited Trauma

Aron Hirt-Manheimer

AND **Marty Yura**

[M]

MANDEL VILAR PRESS

Copyright © 2025 by Aron Hirt-Manheimer and Marty Yura

All rights reserved. No portion of this book may be reproduced in any form or by any means, including electronic storage and retrieval systems, except by explicit prior written permission of the publisher. Brief passages may be excerpted for review and critical purposes.

This book is typeset in Adobe Caslon Pro 11/16. The paper used in this book meets the minimum requirements of ANSI/NISO Z39.48-1992 (R1997). ∞

Text and cover designed by Sophie Appel

Copyedited by Mary Beth Hinton

Unless otherwise noted, photos are from the personal collection of the authors.

Library of Congress Cataloging-in-Publication Data available upon request.

ISBN 978-1-942134-13-8

Printed in the United States of America
25 26 27 28 29 30 31 32 33 34 35 / 9 8 7 6 5 4 3 2 1

Mandel Vilar Press
Simsbury, Connecticut
www.americasforconservation.org | www.mvpublishers.org

contents

Foreword
VII

Prologue
The Poker Game: No Coincidences in Life
XIII

Chapter 1
The Early Years: Making Good in America
1

Chapter 2
A Beautiful Friendship: Our Teen Years in LA
34

Chapter 3
Love and War: College, Israel, and Back
46

Chapter 4
Finding Our Way: Career, Marriage, and Loss
87

Chapter 5
Bearing Witness: Uncovering Our Parents' Pasts
119

Epilogue
A Legacy of Love Against Hate
157

Acknowledgments
163

foreword

Dr. Yael Danieli

This dual memoir presents us with remarkably intimate and candid portraits of two life-long friends coming of age in the tight-knit community of Holocaust survivors in America. Exploring the impacts of their second-generation roots and upbringing, one sees that their modes of expression are different. Aron draws on his experience as an investigative journalist, while Marty applies the empathic skills of a trained psychologist. Part of the joy of reading this book is experiencing the distinct, yet equally compelling, voices and images of these two protagonists, illustrated in these parallel examples.

Aron imagines the annihilation of his relatives in "The Dream."

I am at the Auschwitz-Birkenau extermination complex. At my feet are stone steps leading down to the gas chamber. Without a hint of fear, I descend and push open a steel door. I am met with a burst of radiant light. I become pure energy, at one with the universe, transcending space and time.

I awoke feeling calm but unclear about the dream's meaning. Was it a way of getting closer to the grandparents, aunts, and uncles whose earthly lives had ended in a gas chamber? Was it an unconscious wish that their deaths were not as horrific as I had always imagined—that their souls found peace in the world to come? Was it to ease my own fear of death?

Marty ponders unanswerable questions while on a Zen Peacemakers immersion retreat at the Auschwitz-Birkenau death camp.

An electrified fence surrounded the camp perimeter. How easy it would have been for prisoners to throw themselves against the barrier and end it all. Had I been a prisoner here, would I have flung myself onto the fence? Would I have been able to survive? Perhaps asking myself these lingering questions was a way of putting myself in my father's place when he was confronted daily with life and death choices as a captive.

For many children of survivors, knowing what their families experienced is paradoxically a source of both horror and comfort. Marty "wished to know and to not know."

"I sometimes regret not having asked my parents about their lives before the war," writes Marty, "how they survived, how they found the courage to reconstruct their lives after the war. Yet, I instinctively avoided going down that terrible tunnel. I didn't want to know more than I could handle."

One of the challenges confronting children of survivors is how to contain the multiplicity and intensity of contradictory emotions they experience.

"One evening at our weekly family Shabbat dinner," writes Aron, "I looked across the table and took delight in the sparkle in our grandchildren's eyes as Judy lit the candles. I was suddenly struck with the terrible thought that one and a half million children just like them were slaughtered in Europe for no reason other than having been born Jewish. I kept this fleeting thought to myself and moved on, trying to enjoy the rest of the evening. Moments of joy sometimes trigger feelings of great sorrow in me."

In the process of learning the fate of lost family members, descendants of survivors often treasure every shred of history they discover, however symbolic.

"After years of searching," writes Aron, "I uncovered a single document referring to Piniek [his murdered uncle] in the vast Holocaust archives located in Arolsen, Germany. It noted that Pinkus Mannheimer was born February 11, 1918, and died April 17, 1945. This rare fragment is as meaningful to me as a gravestone."

Making peace with intergenerational legacies of trauma involves a continuous unraveling and acceptance of unbearable memories, emotions, and choices while moving toward liberation and self-actualization. This is what the authors do as they navigate their quest to better understand how the Holocaust impacted their identities and relationships.

The core, perhaps unconscious, motivation of the second generation is to undo and repair the past and heal the world for their parents and themselves (*tikkun olam*, repairing the world).

"The Zen Peacemakers experience," writes Marty, "shifted my focus from pondering whether I would have survived to how I could take loving action in pursuit of a more peaceful world. Having no simple formula for achieving this task, I found comfort in the words of the rabbinic sage Rabbi Tarfon: "You are not obliged to complete the work of repairing the world, but neither are you free to desist from it."

Their parents' adaptational styles used different strategies. Marty set out knowing almost nothing about his parents' wartime experiences, a taboo subject in their home.

"My parents and other family members conspired to keep me in the dark," writes Marty. "They wanted to spare me from knowing about a great calamity I was too young to grasp. Despite their efforts to shield me, I was always aware of the suffering Hitler had inflicted on my family. It was as real as the unspoken number tattooed on my father's arm."

"My parents believed that it was best not to draw a curtain around the subject," writes Aron, "to let my sister and me know from a tender age about the terrible suffering and losses they had endured."

But Aron and his sister ended up with only selective and fragmentary memories, nonetheless.

I first met Aron when he interviewed me for the Winter 2009 edition of *Reform Judaism* magazine on the multigenerational effects of trauma. We connected again in the aftermath of the October 7, 2023, Hamas attack on Israel, when he was a panelist on ICMGLT's (International Center for Multigenerational Legacies of Trauma) May 6, 2024, webinar, "Commemorating and Mourning the Shoah After October 7."

Months later, as we were about to discuss the direction of this book's foreword, Hamas released three barely recognizable, gaunt Israeli hostages. Like many, I was witnessing in utter anguish how reminiscent they were of the emaciated bodies of Holocaust survivors on the day of their liberation. I thought of Aron's description of his father shortly after being liberated from Mauthausen:

> Pop went for a walk in a nearby village with his friend Moniek. Pop stopped in front of a shop and looked at his reflection in the window. Peering back at him was this strange fellow with a crazed look, his body little more than bones. He asked Moniek, "Who's this man staring at me?" Moniek said, "Wolf, that's you."
>
> Pop described how he felt at that moment: "I looked again and could see nothing familiar about this man. How is it possible for a human being to change so much? I was such a strong man. I sat down on the curb and wept like a baby. I had nothing in the world, no family, not even myself."

And yet, after miraculously reuniting with Aron's mother, to whom he was engaged before they became prisoners in different concentration camps, he was able to build a new life, sharing the belief that love cures both the beloved and the one who loves.

Both Marty and Aron received the gift of love from their parents. Their memoir is an expression of their parents' survival and courage in choosing to give the world another chance. It is also their way of sharing that love with us.

"I am in awe of my parents," writes Marty, "and of other survivors who expressed no desire for revenge against Germans or others complicit in the genocidal crimes perpetrated against them.

Our parents mastered the art of living with trauma through their love for each other and for their children. Though Aron and I inherited the pain and sorrow they lived with, we and our children are also heirs to their qualities of love, kindness, and compassion."

"The one constant in my life as a son of a survivor," writes Aron, "is the boundless love that my parents bestowed on Rose and me. Despite all the hatred they endured, or perhaps because of it, they impressed upon us that goodness ultimately will prevail over evil. As Ma put it, 'No bad person wins in the end. What did Hitler achieve?'"

Sons of Survivors is a testament to the power of love against hate.

Dr. Yael Danieli is a clinical psychologist in private practice, a traumatologist, victimologist, and psychohistorian. She is the director of the Group Project for Holocaust Survivors and their Children and founder of the International Center for the Study, Prevention and Treatment of Multigenerational Legacies of Trauma.

— *prologue* —

The Poker Game

No Coincidences in Life

— *aron* —

It was the summer before my senior year at Fairfax High. I spent most of my days catching the sun at Santa Monica Beach, bodysurfing, and working on my tan. Nights were for getting out of the house and having fun. On this particular evening, a game of five-card stud beckoned at the apartment of my buddy Louie Kmiotek. The year was 1965.

— *marty* —

I had just moved to Los Angeles from the Bronx and it was decided my best bet for making new friends was enrolling in summer school. No such luck. It was a complete drag. Plan B was getting to know kids my age in the survivor community. That's what led me to Louie Kmiotek. What impressed me most about Louie was that he was about my age and already driving a brand-new yellow Pontiac GTO.

— *aron* —

Louie wore thick glasses and seemed to have a predilection for Mister Rogers-style alpaca sweaters. His shirts and pants never knew a wrinkle. Seemed that Louie was being groomed to be a *macher*, a big shot, in business like his dad who owned a chain of automated car washes.

I was not into gambling and don't remember how I heard about the poker game. Nor do I have any recollection of whether I won or lost money. But I did gain a new friend.

I took an immediate liking to Marty. He was congenial and good looking—tall, blond hair, blue eyes, stylishly dressed, sleeves folded back with origami-like precision.

After the last hand, I turned to Marty and said, "Can I give you a ride home on my bike?" "Sure," he said enthusiastically. When he saw that it was a dinky little bicycle with a banana seat, he laughed.

— *marty* —

I wasn't really into poker but mustered up the courage to find my way to Louie's apartment. That's where I met Aron. He was a handsome kid and, as I would soon discover, had a good sense of humor. His invitation to give me a ride home on his "bike" led me to think that I was about to have a little thrill on a motorcycle. Nope. It was a bicycle.

— *aron* —

We walked together for a few blocks until we reached 920 North Spaulding Avenue. To our surprise, he lived in the adjacent building. I had a hunch that we would become good friends. As we parted, the hit song, "Boy from New York City," popped into my head: "Ooh wah, ooh wah, cool, cool kitty / Tell us about the boy from New York City."

— *marty* —

The proximity of our apartments made it almost like we were inhabiting the same space. I felt at home around Aron's family. Yiddish was spoken in both our homes. These were my people. To this day, Aron's mother, Adela, talks about how much she appreciated my father's frequent invitations to come next door for a cup of coffee. It was almost as if Aron and I had grown up in the same family. We became like brothers.

— aron —

I felt comfortable around Marty's parents, Jerry and Sophie. They were so much like mine. Though Marty and I were acutely aware of the trauma experienced by our fathers and mothers and their circle of friends in the Holocaust, we didn't really talk about it back then. It was the sixties—sex, drugs, and rock 'n' roll.

—marty —

Aron and I had many adventures together, like driving down to Ensenada, Mexico, in a mural-covered VW van, along with our buddy, Zamir Tarmu, and five members of his funk jazz band. By the time Aron and I graduated from Fairfax High in January 1966 and entered UCLA, we were inseparable.

— aron —

We both majored in psychology and shared an off-campus apartment. Toward the end of our sophomore year, I told Marty that I was signing up for a junior year abroad program at Tel Aviv University. He enrolled in the program as well. After returning home and graduating from UCLA, we both immigrated to Israel.

— marty —

Eventually Aron and I drifted apart. He fell in love with a beautiful Canadian woman he had met in Jerusalem. I joined the Israel Defense Forces.

— aron —

We both moved back to the United States, got married, and started families—Marty in the South and I in the Northeast. Long periods passed without us having much contact. Then something strange happened.

About five years ago I got a call from my daughter, Mimi, who was stranded at the Atlanta airport on Christmas Eve with her husband and their toddler son. Heavy rains had caused the cancellation of all connecting flights. Mimi asked me what to do. I suggested she call my friend Marty, who lived in Atlanta. Marty came to their rescue. The following day Mimi told us how warmly they were embraced and how much "the atmosphere of the Yura home is just like yours." She couldn't understand why we didn't ever get together.

Two months later, Judy and I met Marty and his wife, Marti, at a Manhattan patisserie, breathing new life into our relationship. The next time I saw Marty was in Los Angeles when he made a surprise appearance at my mother's door. He had flown in from Atlanta to celebrate my seventieth birthday.

— *marty* —

I believe there are no coincidences in life. When Aron and I seemingly serendipitously reconnected a few years ago, we were able to re-embrace powerfully. We started having phone conversations and for the first time addressed our shared Holocaust legacies as sons of survivors.

— *aron* —

We learned we were both conceived in Feldafing, a displaced persons (DP) camp in US-occupied Germany. Our fathers had both lived in the same Polish town and had Auschwitz prisoner numbers tattooed on their left forearms. Our mothers had both toiled in the same chain of German slave labor camps. And when they finally made it to America, both our families came through New York Harbor before eventually finding their way to Los Angeles.

— *marty* —

We discussed how our parents had followed divergent strategies in revealing what happened to them and their loved ones during the Holocaust. My parents and other family members conspired to keep me in the dark. They wanted to spare me from knowing about a great calamity I was too young to grasp. Despite their efforts to shield me, I was always aware of the suffering Hitler had inflicted on my family. It was as real as the unspoken number tattooed on my father's arm.

— *aron* —

My parents believed that it was best not to draw a curtain around the subject, to let my sister and me know from a tender age about the terrible suffering and losses they had endured.

— *marty* —

Though our parents had different ways of coping with the tragedies they experienced, in both our cases their intention was to put the past behind them and move forward with their lives, choosing light over darkness, love over hate.

— *aron* —

Sixty years after Marty and I met at that poker game, we decided to traverse the haunted terrain of the Holocaust together. Along the way, we each discovered things we didn't know about our parents and the family members we never had the chance to meet. We emerged with a deeper understanding of how our second-generation Holocaust legacy has informed every stage of our lives and has also impacted our children and grandchildren. Most of all, we grew to appreciate how our parents had endowed us with the ability to transform trauma into a force for living our best lives.

This is our story.

aron's family tree

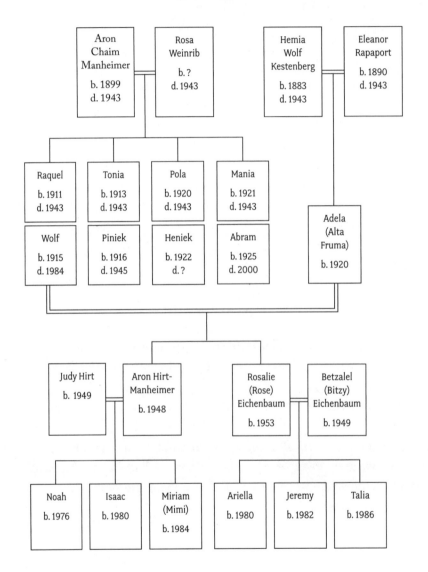

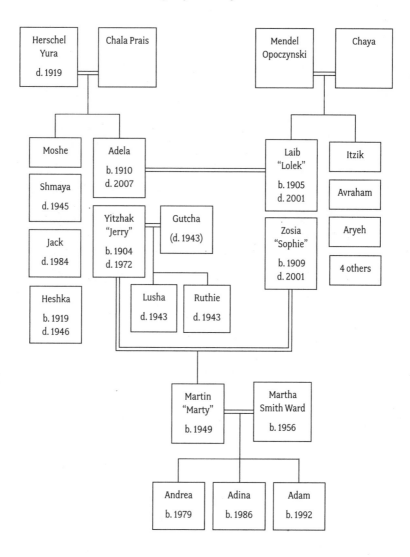

chapter one

The Early Years

Making Good in America

— *aron* —

The Party: How Adela Met Wolf

Tragedy struck my mother's family long before the Nazis invaded Poland.

Her parents, Eleanor and Hemia Kestenberg, had lost a son and daughter to scarlet fever in 1910. Ten years later, as the Great Flu of 1918 was winding down, my mother was born. The Kestenbergs sought the advice of their Hasidic rebbe. "How can we guard our baby against the insatiable *Malach Ha-mavet*, the Angel of Death?"

"Here is what you need to do," the rebbe advised, "Name her Alta Fruma (old pious one). When reporting her date of birth, do not count the first year. For the first seven years of her life, dress her only in white and hang a leather pouch containing a live spider and quicksilver from her neck. They followed the rebbe's prescription scrupulously and Alta Fruma, or Adela, as her friends called her, grew into a young woman.

The Kestenbergs lived at 25 Lukasinskiego Street in Dabrowa Gornicza in the Silesian province of Poland. Every so often Adela would take a bus to Bedzin (Bendin in Yiddish), a nearby mining and manufacturing center. There she would purchase thread, fabric, linings, and other supplies for her father's tailor shop. On one such visit, a girlfriend invited Adela to a party. Wolf Manheimer was among the handful of guests. Adela was twenty-one, Wolf, twenty-six. She liked the way he looked, his black hair and blue eyes. They danced. The year was 1941. The Germans had occupied Poland two years earlier.

The following day, Wolf sent Adela a message via a Dabrowa man who worked in the metal works factory that Wolf operated with his three younger brothers, Piniek, Heniek, and Abram. Wolf wanted to know if she wanted to stay in contact. She replied, "Yes."

After several more communications in this manner, Adela informed her father that she had met a nice guy in Bedzin. She dared not reveal that they had danced. Orthodox Jewish tradition forbids a man to touch a woman who is not his wife. For this offense Wolf might easily have been disqualified as a potential *shidduch*, marital match, for the Kestenbergs' only child. Marriage had been a thorny issue in the Kestenberg home. When Adela turned thirteen, her father called in a matchmaker. "I am too young," Adela protested. Unable to shake her resolve, he relented.

There was no better place than the *mikveh*, the communal ritual bathhouse, for Adela's father to catch up on the local gossip. On his next visit to the *mikveh*, he inquired about the reputation of the Manheimers of Bedzin. To his delight, he learned that Wolf's father, Aron Chaim, was accorded near rabbinic status for his piety and exceptional Jewish scholarship. Not only that. Aron Chaim and his four sons were known for singing liturgical songs in synagogue on Shabbat and that Wolf had an exceptionally beautiful voice. That was all Adela's father needed to hear to sanction the *shidduch*.

Aron Chaim communicated his approval of the match to the Kestenbergs in a perfectly composed letter in Polish. Adela was especially pleased with the letter because she could use it to support her position in an ongoing disagreement with her father, who forbade Polish to be spoken in the house. "We have our own language," he insisted. Adela countered, "We live in Poland, so I should be allowed to speak with my friends in Polish."

To this day, my mother loves to quote Polish aphorisms, though her appreciation of the Polish language was marred by the actions of the Polish kids who called her "dirty Jew" and pelted her with rocks as she walked to school.

The Early Years

Wolf and Adela celebrated their *tnoyim*, wedding engagement, on January 29, 1942, in Dabrowa. When the two were alone for a few minutes in the stairwell, Wolf tried to sneak a kiss. Adela would have none of it, insisting that such things would have to wait until they were wed.

A second engagement party was scheduled for the following week at the Manheimer home in Bedzin. All the festive foods, from the herring to the beer, had been ordered. The celebration did not happen. The Nazis rounded up Adela along with hundreds of other young Jewish women and concentrated them in the nearby town of Sosnowiec. From there she was transported more than 500 miles to Grünberg, a slave labor camp in Schlesien, Germany.

The Pact: How Sophie Met Jerry

My mother, Sophie, was born and lived in Sosnowiec, Poland, about two miles from Bedzin, where my father, Jerry, would eventually take up residence. Originally from Projowiecz, he spent his early years moving from town to town as part of his parents' strategy to keep their five sons—Moishe, Shmaya, Jack, Jerry, and Heshka—from being conscripted into the Polish Army. My father was not passed over. He served in the Polish Army from 1925 to 1927 and reached the rank of sergeant.

Although my father later had a prominent position in Bedzin as the manager of a social club, I don't recall him or Aron's father ever mentioning that they had met one another before we became neighbors in Los Angeles.

The circumstances leading to my parents' engagement were unusual. In one of five camps in which my mother, Sophie, was enslaved during the war, she befriended a woman from Bedzin named Adele (not to be confused with Aron's mother). When the two women learned that each had a brother, they made a pact. If all four of them survived, my mother would introduce Adele to her brother Lolek, and Adele would introduce my mother to her brother Jerry.

After the liberation, networks for verifying who was still alive were widespread but incomplete. Adele traveled by train alone and penniless looking for her brother Jerry in Bedzin only to learn that he was bedridden with typhus in a Czech hospital. She then continued on to Czechoslavakia. For a Jewish woman, this was a tremendously courageous act. I'll always remember her stories of how gracious and helpful the Czech people were along the way, giving her food and shelter. Upon arriving at the hospital, she learned that Jerry had been released just a day earlier. She returned to Bedzin. It was not the same place postwar. The properties of Jews who had been sent to concentration camps were now occupied by Poles. For survivors, the only reason to return to their places of birth was to go through lists of public postings left by others who had come back after the war in search of missing relatives.

Adele finally reunited with Jerry in Bedzin. Sophie found Lolek there as well. Against all odds, the four of them had survived. The pact was honored.

— *aron* —

A Ruth and Naomi Moment

To keep his eldest son out of the Polish Army, Aron Chaim tied Wolf's big toe over the next one until the two overlapped and the string was no longer necessary. That gambit might have worked in the past, but in the face of the German invasion of Poland, Wolf was called up for military duty.

Wolf observed how Polish commanders were positioning Jewish soldiers on the front lines to take the brunt of the German assault. Not about to allow himself to be cannon fodder, he hid in the woods, buried his uniform, and returned to Bedzin. Germany conquered Poland in five weeks. Wolf lived with crossed toes for the rest of his life.

When Adela arrived in the Grünberg concentration camp, the *Betriebsleiter*, factory director, asked the assembled Jewish women, "Who wants to go home?" Adela naively raised her hand. "I'm an only child and my parents need me," she pleaded. The *Betriebsleiter*, a tall, slender man who sported a heavy signet ring, walked up to Adela and punched her in the eye. It was swollen for a month. This was her introduction to the horrors awaiting her as a disposable slave.

The Early Years

Adela found solace in keeping close a portrait of her mother, though she knew that any slave worker hiding a photo would be condemned to death in Auschwitz. One morning the camp guards conducted a surprise body search in the shower room. She swallowed her most precious possession.

Wolf sent Adela packages containing bread and other provisions. Not a crumb ever reached her. In one package, he included an electric iron made in his metal shop in the hope of bribing the *Judenalteste*, the senior Jewess in charge of the group. It didn't help. His fiancée received no preferential treatment.

About a thousand Jewish women labored in a state-of-the-art factory in Grünberg. They produced blankets for the Wehrmacht, the armed forces of Nazi Germany. My mother worked the night shift in the *Spinnerei*, the spinning mill. Operating a complex industrial machine was a high-risk job because any mechanical malfunction was deemed a sabotage, punishable by death. No machine ever broke down on my mother's watch.

After their twelve-hour shift, workers were confined to lice-infested barracks. My mother shared a bunk and blanket with Tzipora Magerkewicz, also from Dabrowa, whom she had met in Sosnowiec before their deportation. Adela had looked around for "a nice girl" to pair up with and chose Tzipora. They became "like sisters" and three years later would escape together from what I later learned was one of the most notorious Nazi death marches.

After the liberation, the first order of business for most survivors was to look for their loved ones. Some traveled back to their hometowns, checked lists, and logged in their names and the names of those they were seeking. Sala Teichner, one of Adela's friends, traveled to Bedzin and came back with news that Wolf was alive in a Paris hospital. His only surviving brother, Abram, having no travel papers, managed to hide himself on a train bound for the French capital. He located his brother and smuggled him into Germany, where Wolf was admitted to a TB sanitorium in Gauting.

A few days later, Adela traveled to Gauting from the Feldafing Displaced Persons Camp to visit Wolf. She sat down next to her betrothed. He looked at her and said, "Hear me. I came out sick. You will never be happy if you stay with me. Your life will be too hard. Forget about the engagement." Adela describes her response as a "Ruth and Naomi moment": *"Vos vet zayn mit deer vet zayn mit meer."* (What will be with you will be with me.)

Adela slept in the wives' barrack on the sanitorium grounds. She volunteered to mend the patients' clothes. Ignoring doctors' warnings not to risk exposure to the highly contagious disease, she looked after all twelve of the men in the ward—without getting sick! For his part, Wolf raised the spirits of his fellow patients by entertaining them with familiar Jewish songs on a small accordion.

On March 30, 1947, Wolf and Adela were married under a *chuppah*, wedding canopy, outside Block 5c Z in the Feldafing Displaced Persons Camp. Adela wore a borrowed wedding dress and veil she had bartered for a bag of oatmeal. Abram procured a respectable suit and tie for Wolf.

Nine months later, my first day was almost my last. Ma's water broke. The camp's only doctor could not be reached for hours. When the doctor finally arrived, he went into emergency mode, practically tearing me out of the womb. Ma remained in the hospital for many days. She was delighted that I had Pop's black hair and blue eyes but was disappointed when my eye color changed from blue to hazel. How could I?

— *marty* —

Feldafing Farewell

Having reunited and introduced each other to their siblings, my parents and future aunt and uncle ended up in the displaced persons camp in Feldafing, Germany. It's where Jerry and Sophie were married, and I was conceived.

DP camps held the record at the time for the highest birth rate of any Jewish community in the world. Having lost five or more years of their lives in hiding or enslavement, many survivors were eager to start a family. In Feldafing alone, with a Jewish population of about 4,000, a whopping seven hundred babies were born between 1945 and 1951!

The American-run DP camp management assigned my father the enviable job of processing and approving visa applications to the United States. A robust black-market economy existed in many of these camps, and some survivors in leadership positions enriched themselves by accepting bribes. When I learned that my father never took even the smallest gift in exchange for issuing visas, my first thought was that our lives would have been so different had we not arrived in the US penniless. I got over my resentment when I realized what an extraordinary moral stand he had taken. For Jerry Yura it was never about money or looking out only for himself. It was all about helping people.

I arrived in New York in utero and was delivered on American soil. My aunt Adele, whom I have called "Aga" since I was a baby, and Uncle Lolek immigrated a short time later, joining us in the Bronx. I vaguely remember their wedding party in our living room, rocking my head from side to side to the music.

— *aron* —

Coming to America

I have no memory of my toddlerhood in Germany. Three small black and white snapshots show a happy little boy playing on the grass of a fenced-in yard. In one of the photos I am running mischievously away from my mother, who is rising from a seated position to chase after me. She is laughing in what I imagine was for her a rare moment of pure joy.

She was right to keep a close eye on me. At age two, I ventured out into the world on my own. A search party caught up with me at a carnival across a busy avenue. What they said about me following that incident has stuck: "*Er hot mer mazel vee farshtand*" (He has more luck than understanding).

My parents had their hearts set on living in *Eretz Yisrael*, the Land of Israel. As teens, Pop and a friend set off on their bikes for Palestine. They managed to get as far as the Italian border before guards turned them back. No papers.

After the war, when Ma and Tzipora Magerkewicz, her "survivor sister," were about to board a ship bound for Palestine, Ma received news that Wolf Manheimer was alive. Ma stayed behind. The ship carrying Tzipora was intercepted by the Royal Navy and the passengers imprisoned in a British concentration camp on the Island of Cyprus. Tzipora would spend another year behind barbed wire before reuniting with her brother in the Promised Land.

In DP camp questionnaires, my parents listed "Palestine" as their desired destination. When the time came to emigrate, survivor friends cautioned that my father was not well enough to withstand the harsh living conditions in the fledgling Jewish state. That is how we ended up going to America.

US immigration officials required my father to present documentation certifying that he was fully cured. In a letter dated May 4, 1951, TB Control Officer Dr. W. Trenkuer wrote: "Mr. Manheimer's condition after thoracoplasty on the right side [shows that] the pulmonary process has healed . . . and there is no evidence of activity." With the last hurdle cleared, we received our visas and on August 28, 1951, boarded a decommissioned US Navy vessel, the USNS *General M. B. Stewart*, in Bremerhaven, Germany, for the twelve-day voyage to America.

Abram had immigrated to Argentina via Paraguay three years earlier with his wife, Clara Frieda Rosenberg, a native of Czechoslovakia whom he had met in Auschwitz, and their two-year-old daughter Dora Rosa. They were greeted by an uncle with the same name as my father, Wolf Manheimer, who set up Abram as a furrier in Buenos Aires. Their second daughter, Raquel, was born the same year my family immigrated to the United States. The brothers would not see one another again for ten years. I later discovered the cause of their living a continent apart.

When our ship docked in New York Harbor, I went missing again. Ma cried out hysterically. "Where is my son? Where is Aron?" I was on the upper deck surrounded by a news crew. They had snatched me for a photo op. Who could blame them? My parents had dressed their three-year-old in Bavarian lederhosen topped off with a little green Tyrolean hat—the perfect refugee poster child.

The next shock came when immigration officials informed my parents that our final destination would be Cleveland. Ma cried out, "Cleve-Land ... But I thought we were coming to America!"

— *marty* —

Smothered in Jewish Mothering

We arrived in New York City in the spring of 1949. At the time, my mother was about three months pregnant with me. Unlike Aron's family, ours was not alone in America.

Our extended immigrant family included members who had left Poland before Hitler rose to power in Germany. My mother's older brothers, Abe and Itzik, each lived with their wives in Queens and the Bronx. My father's older brother, Jack, lived in Los Angeles with his American-born wife, Lilly, who had traveled to Poland in the early 1930s to find a suitable husband. All the men in our family worked long hours, mostly in the garment industry.

Thanks to Uncle Izzy and Aunt Yetta, who had intervened with their kindhearted Jewish landlord, we moved into an affordable fourth-floor walk-up in the Bronx at 1892 Morris Avenue. Uncle Izzy had been married to one of my mother's sisters, who perished in the Holocaust.

Whenever I returned home after stepping out, I was obliged to stop in the stairwell and check in with Aunt Aga, who lived with Uncle Lolek on the first floor. Aunt Yetta greeted me on the second floor, and my mother waited for me on the fourth. I felt smothered in Jewish mothering.

The closeness of our family relationships varied. Uncle Itzik, one of the kindest human beings I've ever known, and his wife, Manya, were welcoming and helpful. They lived a short bus ride away from us in the Bronx. When we visited, Aunt Manya, the rebel in our family, invariably served me a ham sandwich. Tasting this delicious *traif* (forbidden) food for the first time left me wanting more. I pestered my mother until she acquiesced and added ham to my lunch menu.

We didn't find Uncle Abe and his American-born Jewish wife, Helen, particularly warm or welcoming. They never came to visit us. To see them we had to *schlep* by train to Long Island. Abe was heavy-set and amicable. Helen was slim and dour. Like many American Jews of that time, Helen was uncomfortable around "*greeneh*"—refugees who bore the emotional scars of the Holocaust. That is one of the reasons why many survivors kept to themselves. I did not enjoy being around Abe and Helen, and I suspect my parents shared my discomfort.

My parents reminisced nostalgically with Aga and Lolek about their youth. I don't recall such talk among my uncles and aunts who had left Poland before the war. I suppose that having chosen to leave the Old World for a better life in America, they wanted to distance themselves from the past, whereas for the survivors, their prewar lives had been full of promise.

My father's younger brother, Heshka, immigrated to America about the same time we did. He married Bronka, and they had two children: Rita, born in Feldafing, and Irving, born in America. I thought of Rita, who was two and half years older than me, and Irving, just nine months older, as siblings. When our families got together, Rita refused to play with Irving and me. We would try to outdo one another in upsetting her and our parents. I think our families would have gotten together more often had it not been for our rambunctious behavior. We just loved the attention.

Rita and Irving had been instructed never to bring up my father's past. But there was no taboo on mocking our elders for their Old-World mannerisms and outdated child-rearing methods. We ignored their incessant safety warnings before every activity and cracked up every time Heshka cautioned: "*Meh tunisht!*" (One mustn't!)

— *aron* —

Clueless in Cleveland

Having no relatives in America, we were in the hands of the Hebrew Immigration Aid Society (HIAS), which placed us temporarily in the home of a volunteer Jewish family in Cleveland, Ohio. After a few weeks, HIAS relocated us to a four-unit apartment building on Born Avenue in a working-class neighborhood on the east side.

Above us lived a woman with twelve cats. My parents warned me to stay away from those creatures. "They'll scratch your eyes out!" Two survivor families lived in the remaining apartments. The Wieders had a lovely daughter my age named Leah. The other, who shall remain unnamed, was headed by an abusive husband who beat his wife. We felt sorry for her and their two sons.

Our backyard was covered in broken bottles and other debris. One day our landlord showed up and organized the neighborhood kids into a clean-up crew. As we gathered up the scattered litter, he dispensed shiny nickels and dimes—my first job at age six.

Across the street stood an empty lot. I watched with excitement as workmen put up a large tent. I prayed for a carnival and instead got a church. I ventured inside the tent and was swept into the swing of a sizzling gospel choir. The next time I got so high on music was watching the 1954 movie *Rock Around the Clock*, featuring Bill Haley & His Comets. We kids all jumped out of our seats and danced in the aisles.

To make ends meet, Ma offered room and board to Phillip Raucher, a survivor friend who was single. When my sister, Rosalie, was born on June 4, 1953, we needed his room. As a parting gift, Phillip gave us our first store-bought toys: a cap gun for me and a doll for Rose.

My most prized possession was a half blue, half green bike that Pop had pieced together from spare parts. One day my best friend Michael Gordon and I were riding our bikes in a nearby park when a gang of about fifteen kids came rushing down a hill toward us. Mike wisely fled, never again seeing his brand-new bike. I took a few punches in the stomach but refused to let go of mine. They let me keep it.

A Jewish charity would occasionally leave large cardboard boxes full of stuff on our front porch. Rummaging through the assorted kitchenware, linens, clothes, and such was like a treasure hunt. My entire wardrobe, if you could call it that, was made up of hand-me-downs, what some would call *shmates*, rags. But I didn't feel deprived. I had no inkling that we were poor.

My first time away from home was at an overnight Jewish camp on the Lake Erie shore. One day I got wind of something exciting happening outside. Two boys were incinerating a pair of blue jeans in a metal barrel. I joined in the fun, only to discover later that my only pair of long pants had gone missing!

I didn't realize at the time that my Camp Wise bunkmates were playing a prank on a clueless refugee kid.

The Bronx

Our brick building was a block off the landmark Grand Concourse. I'd often look out of my parents' bedroom window through the steps of the fire escape, "our balcony," to see what the neighbors were up to and the action on the street below. Like clockwork, every Sunday morning worshipers set out for mass at St. Margaret Mary Catholic Church. Within a two-block radius, we also had a Protestant church and two synagogues.

I spent all my free time with friends on the street. We played right in the middle of Morris Avenue, as well as in the schoolyard of Wade Junior High School. If I wanted to get hold of a buddy—Neil, David, Spitz, Jeffrey, or Barry—I'd go to their building and shout their name until they came to the window. Everyone knew who the "bad" kids were. We'd see them get stopped by the cops. We rarely got into trouble on the streets. For the most part, we just had fun.

If you want to know if someone actually grew up in the Bronx during the 1950s and wasn't bullshitting you, ask them: "What was a home run playing stickball on the street?" The correct answer: hitting the third sewer on a fly ball.

There were different versions of stickball: "fungo," "mush," "off the wall," hitting on one bounce, or two. We also played touch football, off the stoop, Johnny on the pony, ringolevio, hide-and-seek, scully, slug, punchball, and a particularly sadistic game called mumfreeze. The kid who was "it" had to walk among the others, who stood "frozen" like statues, and get punched until he could see who hit him. The kid who was spotted giving the blow then became the victim. Our version was a bit more civilized by limiting the punches to below the neck. Needless to say, Aunt Aga was unaware of this activity!

Other than Uncle Abe and Helen on Long Island, everyone we knew lived in an apartment. Ours was a two-bedroom, and I had my own room. I was around ten when we got our very first new pieces of furniture. Mine included a desk with a chair and a bed with a bookcase headboard. After completing the ninth grade, my parents got me my own portable television set. WOW! I spent every night watching Jack Paar, Steve Allen, and Johnny Carson. TV just sucked me in.

— *aron* —

Sunny Acres

When my parents could no longer stand the odor of cat urine permeating the building, they decided to move. Thanks to *Wiedergutmachung* (to make good again), the German government's 1953 decision to pay reparations to Holocaust survivors, they were able to put a down payment on a duplex about a mile away at 686 East 124th Street. I was excited to be living only a few steps from my new elementary school, Hazeldell.

My parents must have gotten a good deal on the house. Who else would sign an agreement stipulating that it came with a bedridden elderly Scottish woman until death do us part? Ina Cowie resembled George Washington on the dollar bill, only with tinted blue hair and red-rouged cheeks. She rarely left her room, perhaps because she sensed, with good reason, that Rose and I sometimes would search through her belongings. Ma and Pop labeled her an antisemite, which we took as license to tease her or worse, like the time when Rose wouldn't stop crying the first day in kindergarten. Ma had to bring her home before returning to the school herself for a consultation with her teacher. When Ma tried to leave the house, Rose got hysterical and would not let go of Ma's leg. When Ms. Cowie tried to restrain my sister, she bit the old lady's hand.

Adding to Ma's *tsuris*, woes, Pop suffered a recurrence of TB and was hospitalized in Sunny Acres, a ten-building sanitorium on the outskirts of

Cleveland. For the next two years, I was able to visit Pop only once and used the occasion to sing him a song of longing that I composed for the occasion. I didn't think to ever ask Ma or Pop how he contracted tuberculosis in the first place. I had always known him as a sick man. Later, I would learn he committed an act soon after his liberation that would cost him his health.

Convinced that our disagreeable housemate took quiet delight in our misfortune, I told Ms. Cowie a fib: "My father is coming home in two weeks." I must have had a premonition. To my surprise, Pop was discharged exactly two weeks after my pronouncement! A short time later, Ina Cowie died in her bed.

— *marty* —

Germans in the Basement

Mr. Weber, our building's superintendent (super) lived with his wife and two sons in a windowless basement "apartment" amidst all kinds of stored objects. His duties included shoveling coal into the furnace, clearing snow, and responding to emergencies.

I never ever saw Mr. Weber smile. He was a tall man with a grim demeanor. A scar began near his lower lip and extended down the side of his chin. His wife was the only pleasant person in the family.

Uncle Lolek, who would remain bitter and scornful to his dying day, suspected our supe of having a Nazi past. My parents may have shared his suspicion but treated Mr. Weber and his family with kindness and respect. It was their way of putting the past behind and leaning into a new life in America. For me, it was a formative lesson not to see all Germans as bad or evil.

— *aron* —

Pigeons for Yiddish Lessons

Pop couldn't find employment in Cleveland, mostly due to his compromised health. Ma became the breadwinner in our family, working at a neighborhood bakery. On many nights while walking home in the dark laden with unsold loaves of bread, cakes, and pastries, she was forced by local hoods to surrender the goods. Ma's scant earnings barely kept us afloat. Thankfully, our social circle of survivors acted as a kind of mutual aid society.

From time to time, Mr. Rottenberg, a butcher, would bring us packages of meat neatly hand-wrapped in wax paper. One night, he offered my father his old Studebaker. Pop, who had never driven a car, took it out for a spin. He returned home rattled. I looked out the window and saw part of another car hanging from one of the Studebaker's door handles. Never again would Pop sit in the driver's seat.

Pop did most of the cooking and housework. Dinners consisted mostly of broiled burgers, steaks, lamb chops, chicken, or liver with a side of some green vegetable like brussels sprouts. On school days he prepared our lunches and brushed Rose's hair into a ponytail. Ma had to leave early to catch the bus to work. If Pop felt inadequate in any way for having to play the traditional mothering role, he never showed it. He always greeted us with a big smile when we came home from school.

Aside from his household chores, Pop was always thinking about how he could augment Ma's salary. When I was eight or nine, Pop decided to start a home-based costume jewelry business. He ordered various earring components, glued them together, and attached the finished pieces to little squares of white cardboard. One day he called me over and said, "Aron, I need you to go from door to door and sell jewelry." Being an obedient and dutiful son, I put a few handfuls of earring packets into a bag and started knocking on doors.

The jewelry must have been a bargain, or maybe the women who came to the door felt sorry for me; whatever the reason, I came home with a pocket full of cash. I don't know if Pop's venture made a profit, but it certainly energized him. As his next enterprise, Pop sewed up a load of green faux-leather shopping bags. Sales were not very brisk, leaving us with a lifetime supply.

Pop was ready to give up on his money-making schemes when an African American man appeared at our front door with a proposition. He asked Pop to teach him Yiddish. "Why do you want to learn Yiddish?" my father asked. "Because Jews are so successful," he replied. The man said he could only afford to pay in pigeons. I guess a bird in the hand was good enough for Pop.

When I came home from school the next day, Pop handed me a pigeon and a knife. "Aron, "he said, "Go out back and *shekht de toyb* (butcher the pigeon) for dinner." Being an obedient and dutiful son, I did as he asked.

It didn't go well. The knife was too dull for the job. There I was with a half-dead *toyb* on my hands. What to do? After wavering for a few minutes, I tossed the pigeon over the back fence into a neighbor's yard.

I told Pop that the pigeon had escaped. He seemed relieved. The following morning I overheard a neighbor tell someone she had found a wounded bird in her yard and was nursing it back to health.

Fitting In

Although I spoke English at home, my parents communicated among themselves mostly in Yiddish. I understood Yiddish pretty well, so when my relatives wanted to exclude me they switched to Polish.

I wanted to fit in just as much as any other American kid, which is why my parents' foreign accent and awkward phrasing sometimes bothered me. Even worse, at times they had trouble making themselves understood. I had such a moment myself in first grade when I referred to a radiator as "the steam." The quizzical look on everyone's face embarrassed me. For the first time, I felt different from the other students.

After that incident, I avoided calling attention to myself. It got so bad that I didn't raise my hand to ask for permission to go to the bathroom, resorting to peeing in my pants. I refrained from asking questions in class or expressing views that might be challenged. At recess I stayed on the margins, though I really wanted to jump in and play.

In third grade I put off completing a project until the evening before it was due and went into a panic, as if some tragic fate awaited me if I failed to turn it in on time. My parents called in our family's designated intellectual, Uncle Lolek, who helped me avert this impending calamity. To this day, I feel a certain dread of deadlines.

— aron —

The Day I Knocked Out Rose's Front Teeth

If a brother could be a parent too, that would describe my relationship with my sister Rose. I saw my role as her protector, guarding against anyone who might cause her harm.

One day while standing at a crosswalk waiting for the traffic light to turn green, Rose was suddenly pinched hard on her arm by a boy in her class. She yelled, "Ouch," and I punched her assailant right in the nose. "Why'd you hurt my sister?" I demanded. His defense: "She's not wearing green and it's Saint Patrick's Day." He then ran away, fearing that I might hit him again. Rose remembers how shocked she was to witness me being so violent. I surprised myself. What was the root of this anger, this rage?

My sister and I enjoyed each other's company, often making up and playing games together. I never minded her tagging along. When Rose was four, she accompanied me to the nearby schoolyard for some batting practice. As I stepped up to the plate, I didn't notice her behind me crouched in a catcher's stance. When I pulled the bat back for the first swing, I heard a little crunch. I turned around and saw blood trickling from her mouth.

What to do in this situation? Bribery. We headed straight to the local candy store, where I treated Rose to a couple of those long strips of paper dotted with candy buttons. I then chewed a piece of bubble gum and applied it to keep her wobbly front teeth in place. Maybe our parents wouldn't notice. And if they did, we conspired to tell them some neighborhood kid did it.

When we returned home, Ma was on the phone chatting with her friend Helen Schmulewitz. We walked past her nonchalantly, but she noticed something was amiss and summoned Rose to her for a closer look. Then came the universal Yiddish distress call, "*Oy Gevalt!*" followed by the inevitable question, "Who did this to you?" Rose replied, "A boy in the schoolyard."

I was sure that after a year the case would be closed. Nope. One evening, as we sat around the dinner table, Pop suddenly turned to me and said, "It was you who knocked out Rosalie's teeth. Tell the truth." "Yes," I confessed, "I did it, but it was an accident." I couldn't believe that my father had suspected me all along and would still be so angry about the loss of a couple of baby teeth.

In retrospect, I think what had angered Pop more than the deception was my setting a bad example for Rose. I learned my lesson, but what has stayed with me all these years is my sister's devotion to me.

Rose recently told me about a dream she had as a child: "Some Nazi soldiers burst into our house and forced us to stand in front of a brick wall in a dark alley. Then they pulled me out of the line and told me that only one of the three could live and the others would be shot. I was forced to decide who would live. I chose you because I felt that you hadn't lived long enough, and that Ma and Pop had at least made it to adulthood."

— *marty* —

Cautious in the Extreme

Unlike my father, who had a concentration camp number tattooed on his left forearm, my mother had no such identifying symbol. What my mother did have as a "souvenir" of her years as a slave was a foot-long scar diagonally across her upper back. It could have been a whip's marking. I was never clear about the origin of this wound, only that it was related to her time in the camps. I remember not ever wanting to touch it, not because I thought it would hurt her, but because I thought it was "icky."

This reluctance on my part seemed to be emblematic of the separateness between my mother and me. I don't remember going to her for comfort. I mostly kept things to myself. I always felt that she couldn't really understand what I was going through emotionally. I was often short-tempered with her, and also with Aunt Aga. That I got away with this sort of behavior may have been their indulgence of a self-centered only child.

As an adult, I learned that my mother hadn't felt at ease breast-feeding me for fear of dropping me or doing something else that might injure me. This seemed to be how she interacted with life—cautious to an extreme.

Her love for me was never in question. She was always patient with me. At times when I was frustrated doing homework assignments, she lovingly and wisely suggested that I just take a break and come back to the task after a while.

My mother did the best she could. I have sweet memories of us being together on late winter afternoons waiting for my father to return home from work. She and I would sit at a small table in our living room, warmed by the heat from "the steam," assembling small Lego-like red tiles into houses. I felt content, connected, as if we were on the same level, no generational gap, no language challenges, aligned in our desire for my father to return home safely.

— *aron* —

Invisible Chains

For much of her life, Ma saw herself as a victim of a great injustice. This was manifested in equal measures of distrust and caution. As children, Rose and I were instructed never to talk to strangers. If an adult asked us a question, the answer should always be, "I don't know"—with one exception: "How old are you?"

When accompanying Ma to the supermarket, I always felt embarrassed watching her painstakingly examine the cash register receipt. Truth be told, she was overcharged more often than not. Calling the cashier to account was Ma's way of confronting injustice, while teaching me not to be overly trusting.

Freedom from Nazi captivity did not mean psychological liberation. Ma's invisible chains have expressed themselves through seemingly contradictory impulses. She is extremely cautious yet can be overly trusting. She yearns for serenity yet sees life as an unending struggle. She wants to exercise control of her life yet believes that everything is predetermined, "meant to be." All this was disconcerting to me as a child.

— *marty* —
All-American Boy

At age nine I lobbied my parents to let me become a Cub Scout, the most all-American experience I could imagine. The idea of wearing a cool uniform appealed to me almost as much as the idea of making new friends in a new setting. I was alone among my street friends in venturing into this uncharted territory. Cub Scout Pack 28 included boys from all over our section of the Bronx. Some of them lived blocks away, which qualified as a whole other world. My mother dutifully played her role as a den mother, but I could see how awkward she felt.

At age eleven I advanced to Boy Scouts. The participation of dads was practically mandatory. My father, who was considerably older than the others, had little appetite, energy, or patience for camping or any other scouting activities. He certainly didn't share my enthusiasm for uniforms. Most of the other dads were Jewish but showed no interest in hearing about what had happened to their European brethren during the Holocaust.

My crowning achievement was promotion to the leadership of our pack's Cuckoo Patrol, but my primary goal of making new friends was not realized. The kids with the most active fathers were snotty and elitist. I felt tolerated but never fully included. I was most comfortable and at ease with my friends on the street. To this day I'm in regular contact with my best friend at the time, Neil. I couldn't tell you the name of even one boy scout in our pack.

I have grown to appreciate the lengths to which my parents went to help me see myself as a "normal" American boy.

— *aron* —
A Good Boy

My first girlfriend, Leah Wieder, who lived next door on Born Avenue in Cleveland, tells me that at age six I was a "good boy, very quiet and reserved, except for one time." After her family returned from a visit with relatives in New York, Leah became friendly with their son. He gave her a photo of himself. "When I showed it to you, Aron," she recalls, "you got jealous and said, 'I want to rip this up.'"

All my friends in Cleveland were children of survivors. Michael Gordon was the exception. We both attended the same elementary and Hebrew schools. His parents spoke English without foreign accents. Mike's father, Sanford Gordon, was a celebrated rocket scientist for NASA. His mother, Beatrice, had an MA in social work.

Mike and I were in third or fourth grade when he told me that he had been placed in the advanced class. Feeling the sting of jealousy, I griped, "Why you and not me? I'm just as smart." Mike then put me to the test:

"What is Daylight Savings Time?"

"The hours a bank is open during the day."

"Wrong."

"What are Aesop's fables?"

"He was a big liar."

Wrong."

"What is the lesson of George Washington chopping down the cherry tree?"

"Hard work pays off."

"Wrong."

Mike made his point, but at least he should have given me some credit for my creativity!

Mike did better in school, but I had street smarts. I knew how to make a buck. When I asked Mike recently what he remembers about our times together in Cleveland, he said, "At your initiative, we often went bottle hunting together and usually made quite a haul." I invested my share of the bottle-deposit revenue on packs of baseball cards and comic books.

Ask my mother if I was a good boy, and she'll tell you this story: "I offered to buy Aron a toy and he said, 'It's okay, Ma. Buy something for yourself.'" She doesn't talk about the time we were shopping and I pilfered a package of plastic green soldiers. Ma let me keep my little army but warned, "Just wait until your father comes home!"

When Pop learned of my transgression, he cast a threatening look at me and unbuckled his belt. An Abraham-Isaac moment. As he lifted his arm to strike me, my mother screamed out in Polish: "*Nie Mego!*" (Don't do it!) And that was the end of it. Their predictable disciplinary strategy didn't stop me from committing various misdemeanors around the house, like liberating loose change from Pop's jacket in the hall closet. In any case, I felt confident that my parents would never actually hit me. In fact, when my mother got really angry with me, she would break down in tears and punch herself hard on both sides of her head with her fists. There was no worse punishment than having to witness that.

Making a Living

In concentration camp, my mother's prowess as a seamstress helped keep her alive. In the Bronx, she made clothing alterations for neighbors to supplement my father's income. People who saw her work marveled at her "golden fingers." The sequined dress she would design and wear on the occasion of my bar mitzvah was a piece of art.

My father worked as a sewing machine operator in the Manhattan garment district. He was paid by the piece—"piece work." Every weekend my mother would sew small strips of paper called "tickets" onto larger sheets of paper, each representing an item he had stitched the previous week. She wanted to make sure the tickets were clearly and accurately displayed to ensure that her husband was paid fairly.

I used to wonder why my father did this kind of menial work. He seemed capable of so much more. Before the war, he had managed a social club in Bedzin. I imagine that would have been a natural role for such a personable and gracious man. I've been told that he has always made those around him feel happy and at ease.

For my father, success was measured by how well he provided for his family and looked out for the well-being of others, not by how much money he had in the bank.

At some point, he began to work for an immigrant friend, Carl, in what they called a "department store." A long bus ride across the Bronx got you to this place, which was actually a little clothing store crammed with garments, shoes, and a mishmash of other dry goods. Occasionally, my father would bring home a new item of clothing as a surprise gift. Most of my wardrobe was courtesy of Howard Weinberg, a kid who was a year older than me and lived two floors below us.

My father's move from sewing to sales made me feel that our family had risen on the ladder of success, though in my mind it still lacked the cachet of the jobs held by my friends' dads: a New York City sanitation worker and a taxi driver.

None of my street friends were particularly well off, but they all owned nice bikes, all of which at some point were stolen. David had a really cool "Dutch Racer" and Neil sported a three-speed. Thieves didn't bother with my old Schwinn clunker.

There were some things I wanted that my parents couldn't afford. Stickball was my game of choice, but I could only dream of owning a baseball glove or a pair of Converse sneakers. A twenty-six-cent Spalding high-bounce pink rubber ball was out of my league, so I would fish for them in storm drains with a coat hanger. At the candy store, I occasionally bought myself an "egg cream" for seven cents, but never the large size that cost a nickel more. A fifteen-cent slice of pizza or a twenty-cent deli frank or potato knish fell into the category of "approved expenses."

As a young teen, I lobbied my father for a set of barbells, an item that fell into the category "We can't afford this." At one point my pleading so frustrated him that he sat down on my bedroom floor and began beating his fists against the sides of his head. I had never seen him act in such a shocking manner. My selfishness had caused him to lose his cool. The incident taught me that nothing is worth having if it results in the suffering of another person, especially someone you love.

— *aron* —

Bedtime Stories

Pop's bedtime stories portrayed a perilous world—tales of cats scratching out people's eyes, Spanish conquistadors boiled and eaten by cannibals, the Düsseldorf murderer whose head ended up in a guillotine basket.

Even stories about Pop's superhero, Shimshon HaGibor (Samson the Mighty) ended tragically. Born Zishe Breitbart in Lodz, Poland, this daring Jewish circus strongman thrilled audiences with death-defying feats. Pop told me how he witnessed a truck full of elephants driving over boards placed on top of Shimshon's body. He watched as his hero pounded nails into those boards with his bare fist. That act proved to be Shimshon's undoing. After a rusty nail pierced and infected one of his legs, he chose death over amputation.

I never blamed Pop for telling me nightmarish tales. After all, they reflected his life experience. I think he wanted me to be acutely aware of how tenuous life can be—his way of preparing me for the worst.

— *marty* —

Conspiracy of Silence

References to the Holocaust rarely came up in my family. The one exception was when my mother used the shorthand expression, "What Hitler did." My father didn't even go that far, avoiding any mention of his past. The tacit family policy was "Don't ask; don't tell."

I later learned that my family had conspired to keep me in the dark about what they had lived through. They wanted to spare me from knowing about a catastrophe they felt I was too young to grasp. I understood many years later that their strategy also made it easier for them to avoid dealing with their own demons at a time when all their energy was dedicated to the demands of building a new life in America.

Despite my parents' efforts, "What Hitler did" could not be locked away. When I was about six years old, I declared to my family, "When I grow up, I'm going to fly over Germany in an airplane and drop broken glass on them."

I still recall Aunt Aga's quizzical reaction to my uncharacteristic outburst. Any overt sign of anger in our family was quickly quashed. Just as curious was my choice of broken glass, which in our overly cautious family, symbolized imminent danger of injury.

When I was about eight, Uncle Lolek brought out an old photo album. He would point out, person by person, who survived (very few) and who was killed. One picture depicted him sitting with two other young men. He explained that one was his brother and the other a cousin. Without the slightest hint of emotion, he told me that one was shot to death in France and the other in Poland. At the time I didn't quite grasp the gravity of what he was conveying because of his matter-of-fact tone.

Although Aunt Bronka and Cousin Helen had made two separate puzzling references to my father's past, I paid them no mind. Surprised that I didn't know what they were talking about, they quickly dropped the subject. I reasoned that if my father had not told me, perhaps the subject should remain unspoken. I too had learned how to keep silent.

— *aron* —

Living with the Truth

Though the Holocaust was not a taboo subject in our home, Rose and I knew little beyond the fact that Hitler killed many of our relatives and that our parents survived years of frightening and brutal treatment in Nazi concentration camps.

We were familiar with Ma's narrative about how she escaped from a death march and that Pop was shot through the chest by a Nazi sentry after jumping from a train. But we had no idea of exactly how, why, and when these events occurred. Did our parents forget all but a few details or did they not want to dig them up? Pop, I now realize, chose not to talk to me about his Holocaust experiences, and I didn't ask. I was content with the little I knew and wanted to avoid causing him emotional distress.

At the age of four or five, Rose would sit on Pop's lap in our living room and play a game she called "Baby Hand." His hand would be like a puppet that communicated in a kind of sign language. Sometimes Rose would cover the blue-green number, 149719, tattooed on his left forearm and ask him to recite it by memory. Not once did he ever get it wrong.

Rose went to Pop with her problems, like when she came home with a bad report card. He would always take her side, even changing a grade or two before Ma came home from work. Their special relationship might be why she felt more comfortable asking him about the past, and why he revealed more to her than to me.

Even if Ma and Pop had not told us anything about the Holocaust, we would have known that they had experienced terrible traumas. Rose and I sometimes were awakened in the night by the sounds of their night terrors. Signs of Pop's suffering were as conspicuous as his blue eyes. Scars where a bullet had pierced his chest. A large cavity in the right side of his back where seven ribs had been resected as part of a surgery to stem TB. The Auschwitz prisoner tattoo. The permanent blue mark on the middle knuckle of his right hand where a kapo had caned him daily in the Mauthausen concentration camp.

From as early as I can remember, I imagined myself as an avenger bent on tracking down the greatest supervillain of all time, Adolf Hitler, and putting a bullet through his head. Rose's retribution plan came to her in a dream: "Hitler was captured alive and convicted for crimes against humanity. His punishment was to put him on display in a glass tank the size of a small building. A tall ladder was provided for anyone who wanted to climb to the top and spit on him. Hitler drowned in saliva."

— *marty* —

A Most Stylish Captain Hook

When I was in kindergarten at PS28, our class put on a Peter Pan skit. I was cast as Captain Hook. Our teacher asked parents to provide the costumes. On the day of the event my classmates all showed up either in store-bought or flimsily constructed homemade costumes. I walked in wearing a hand-made, custom-tailored, full-length, bright red costume, hook in hand, with a black wig and fancy shoes. Clearly, my mother went all out. Sewing was an art that she had mastered.

For concentration camp inmates, productive work was a matter of life or death. For new immigrants, it was a way of demonstrating their talents. In this case, I think it was more an act of motherly love. I wore my costume proudly, though I was somewhat perplexed that no other parent rose to the occasion.

The Holocaust continued to lurk in the background of my sheltered world until it moved front and center in 1961, when reports on the trial of Adolf Eichmann were aired each evening on WABC TV. I'll forever remember Jim McKay, the TV announcer, and his compassionate reporting.

Following the trial with my mother created a unique opportunity to inquire about her past. I learned that she had survived five different forced labor camps, including Langenbielau (Bielawa) in southwest Poland. From April 1944 until her liberation a year later, she labored there as a seamstress, making and mending military uniforms and parachutes. Her adeptness at sewing earned her additional food rations, which she often shared with Aga and other women prisoners.

One female German guard offered to smuggle my talented mother to her family home in a coffin posing as a corpse. She declined. Way too risky.

Eager to share my mother's story, I received permission to talk about the Holocaust to my sixth-grade class. Each morning, I stood in front of the class, sharing what my mother was telling me. As I spoke, my teacher, Mrs. Arnowich, sat in the back of the room, weeping. I didn't realize then how naturally I had assumed the role of bearing witness.

— *aron* —

Righteous Deeds Rewarded

As a child, I held a certain reverence for the Almighty but doubted that he was actually keeping an eye on me. One day, while riding my bike through a tough Cleveland neighborhood, I decided to utter God's name in vain and braced myself for a divine smack. I made it home without incident, thinking that God must have been attending to more pressing matters that day.

My parents were raised in very religious homes. Pop's father spent his days praying and studying Torah. Many nights he slept on a hard, wooden bench—an ascetic appeal to God to hasten the coming of the Messiah.

Ma's father, Hermia, was a pious tailor who had grown up an orphan and took to heart the religious obligation to welcome the stranger. Every Friday night, he would come home from synagogue accompanied by a poor out-of-town guest. His wife, Eleanor, devoted much of her time and energy to preparing Sabbath meals for these visitors. They all brought happiness—some by coming, others by going. One tried to steal the silverware in the dark of night. A careless smoker nearly burned down the house.

Ma has always believed that God delivered her from Nazi captivity as a reward for her father's righteous deeds. Pop, on the other hand, never ceased being *broiges,* bitterly angry, with the Almighty for allowing such a catastrophe to befall our people.

— *marty* —

Religious School Rebel

When I was seven or eight, my parents sent me to a Yiddish school to acculturate me to their mother tongue and related traditions. I didn't like being ghettoized in that way and convinced them to enroll me in a Jewish school in which Hebrew was taught and where I knew some of the kids.

The move did not stop me from becoming a nuisance. In public school I was restrained and obedient, but in religious school I was a *"farshtunkener,"* translated loosely as a smartass. I dropped water balloons on the younger students as they left the building and, for good measure, assaulted them with my pea shooter. After giving me many warnings, the rabbi expelled me for calling him a "son-of-a-bitch." My father marched me back the next day to apologize, averting the cancellation of my bar mitzvah.

Why was I Dr. Jekyll in public school and Mr. Hyde in religious school? I think the answer lies in my anger at an almighty God for allowing the Holocaust to happen. I suspect that Uncle Lolek's contempt for those who made excuses for God's going AWOL while his "chosen people" were mass murdered had rubbed off on me.

— *aron* —

Rosh Hashanah at the Movies

Though my parents were not particularly observant, they insisted on a religious education for their son. They sent me to an Orthodox-run religious school in Cleveland, where I learned how to sound out the Hebrew alphabet. One of the teachers recognized that I had a good voice and recorded an album of me singing a dozen liturgical and Yiddish songs, which I sweetly dedicated to my parents for their anniversary.

We never belonged to a synagogue, so every year when the High Holy Days rolled around, Pop and I became wandering Jews in search of a house of worship that did not require tickets to enter. Sometimes we would pray in an ultra-Orthodox synagogue in which men and women sat apart and the rabbi was constantly appealing for silence and donations. Once we landed high up in the balcony of the cavernous Reform synagogue Anshe Chesed Fairmount Temple, where we heard our favorite singer, Eddie Fisher, sing the Kol Nidrei prayer.

This pattern of non-affiliation continued after our family moved to Los Angeles when I was eleven years old. One year on the second day of Rosh Hashanah, Pop and I planned to attend services at Temple Israel of Hollywood. We were shocked to find the doors locked. It was news to us that most Reform congregations at the time observed only the first day of this High Holiday.

What would we tell Ma if we returned straight home? To fill the time, Pop took me to see a movie on Hollywood Boulevard. In the darkness, I prayed that God was attending to more pressing matters.

— *marty* —

Praying for the Yankees on Yom Kippur

While studying the Spanish Inquisition in high school, I asked my father what he would have chosen: to denounce Judaism and become a Christian or to refuse and be tortured and burned alive? He said simply, "They should just kill me."

This was a seminal moment for me. I realized that being Jewish defined my father. He could not be anything but a Jew, and it had nothing to do with religious belief. He never talked about God. If religion played any role in his life, it was expressed in terms of being a *mensch*—acting toward others with human decency, kindness, and compassion.

Our home was traditionally Jewish. Before Shabbat dinner on most Friday nights, my mother covered her eyes and recited the blessing over the candles. We skipped the blessings over the wine and challah. Every Pesach, my father and Uncle Lolek alternated as the seder leaders, both racing through the Haggadah readings to hasten the coming of the meal. It's not that my father was unschooled in Jewish ritual and practice. In Poland, both of my parents were raised and educated in Orthodox homes.

I accompanied my father to synagogue three times a year, on the High Holy Days. Most memorable were the men draping their large prayer shawls over their shoulders and heads like a tent and swaying back and forth while reciting the Shema prayer.

The worship services went on for hours, so we kids were reprieved for long stretches of time. While the adults were praying to be sealed in the book of life, we were praying for the Yankees to win the World Series, which often coincided with these holidays. If my father wanted to find me, all he had to do was go down the block to the neighborhood bar where I would be watching the game from outside on their color TV.

— *aron* —

My Five & Ten Bar Mitzvah

Though Pop held a grudge against God, he would never forsake the life-cycle traditions of our people. For a thirteen-year-old boy, not having a bar mitzvah was as unthinkable as not being ritually circumcised on the eighth day of life. Since we didn't belong to a synagogue, my parents had to improvise. They found an elderly man to tutor me in the Fairfax area, a thirty-minute bike ride from our apartment on Wooster Street. Once a week I would sit at his side learning how to recite my Torah portion.

My bar mitzvah was scheduled to take place at Etz Jacob, a large Orthodox synagogue on Beverly Boulevard in West Hollywood. I first met with the rabbi a few days before the event. When he asked me if I had prepared a speech, I said no one had said anything about a speech. He pulled one from a drawer. It was titled, "Bar Mitzvah Prayer." Full of references to our "Heavenly Father," it seemed like an exercise in how many ways one can address the Lord. My tongue got tired of saying, "Thy," "Thee," and "Thine."

I felt very uncomfortable standing on the *bimah*, podium, and much relieved to get it over with. That afternoon, a few family friends gathered in our apartment for bagels, herring, and schnapps. Each guest handed me an envelope containing a five- or ten-dollar bill.

The real Aron was not present at my bar mitzvah. I felt like an imposter going through the motions. The commemorative bar mitzvah portrait of me wearing a *kippah*, skullcap, and *tallit*, prayer shawl, was so heavily touched up that I could hardly recognize myself.

My Marquee Bar Mitzvah

A wave of bar mitzvah celebrations swept through our survivor community in the early sixties. Mine took place on a Saturday morning in an Orthodox synagogue on Walton Avenue in the Bronx. A rabbi had coached me for several months on chanting the Torah and Haftarah portions. Uncle

Lolek helped me prepare an original speech on the Jewish value of compassion toward all living beings.

Cousin Helen attended with her husband, Richard, and their two daughters. She adored Dad, who as I later learned saved her life in Auschwitz by sneaking her food. As I spoke, Helen looked up at me with glistening, tear-filled eyes. She understood how much reaching this day meant for my parents.

The party was held the following Sunday afternoon at Ellesmere Caterers on 170th Street in the Bronx. It was a big deal. I was the "main attraction." Guests could see my name on the marquee above the entrance to the hall. Everyone had a reserved seat marked by a folded place card, and the kids got to sit together at their own large tables.

We had a band, an open bar, hors d'oeuvres, and a three-course meal. We danced the hora, twist, swing, polka, cha-cha-cha, tango, and more. At the designated time, the festivities were paused for the popular ceremony of calling up guests for the honor of lighting a candle on the cake and having their picture taken with the bar mitzvah boy.

What really stood out for me at this event was how thoroughly the survivors enjoyed themselves: hugging, laughing, dancing, feasting, drinking (some to excess). The coming of age of their children was one of the rare times that survivors allowed themselves to let go and publicly acknowledge accomplishments that were unimaginable only a few years earlier.

Gifts at a bar mitzvah most often took the form of a sealed envelope with a check payable either to the center of attention or to the parents. I handed every envelope to my father. I don't know who gave me what or how much. The entire "take" went to just paying for the party.

I remember receiving one non-monetary gift. A survivor from Bedzin named "Yossele" Rosensaft, who wasn't actually among my parents' close circle of friends, mailed it to our house. Opening the package, I was stunned to find inside a Polaroid instant camera. This was an "off the charts" gift. Polaroid cameras were magical, able within a minute to print the picture from the camera itself. I asked my father how his friend could afford such a lavish gift. He explained in a matter-of-fact way that Yossele Rosensaft was a rich man. I could see from the tone of his response that he did not feel inadequate for not having the same wealth as his friend. He was grateful for what he had.

— *aron* —

No Coincidences

It wasn't until we reconnected and started discussing our pasts that Marty mentioned the Polaroid camera he received as a bar mitzvah gift from Yossele Rosensaft. The name sounded familiar. I asked my mother if she knew him. She said, "Of course. He was from Bedzin and after the liberation became a top leader of the survivors. He came several times to the sanitorium in Gauting with food packages for Pop."

That was the first time I heard Marty say, "There are no coincidences in life." I thought of our parents moving to neighboring buildings on North Spaulding Avenue in Los Angeles, setting the stage for their sons to become like brothers.

chapter two

A Beautiful Friendship

Our Teen Years in LA

— *aron* —

Paradise Found

Pop's compromised respiratory system was no match for Cleveland's cold winters and humid summers. When he learned that his father's sister had settled in Los Angeles from Belgium, he wrote to her asking about life in California. "Here is a Paradise," she wrote back, "always warm and sunny."

As winter approached, Pop decided to make an exploratory trip to Los Angeles. He stayed with his aunt and her husband, who lived in the city's fashionable Miracle Mile district. Every day Pop would walk along palm-lined Wilshire Boulevard to a nearby park, site of the La Brea Tar Pits (where many a prehistoric mammoth and saber-toothed tiger had been swallowed up). There he would spend each day sunning himself on a bench. Neither smog nor the smell of petrol wafting from the black bubbling tar pits diminished his rapture. Pop was smelling the roses.

When Pop returned to Cleveland, he announced, "We're moving to Paradise." Rose and I added Al Jolson's "California Here I Come" to our repertoire of songs we were called upon to perform for visiting family friends.

California, here I come
Right back where I started from
Where bowers of flowers bloom in the spring
Each morning at dawning
Birdies sing and everything ...

Open up that Golden Gate
California, here I come!

My parents sold their duplex to a Ukrainian family with the proviso that the buyers could move in with us until we vacated. Ma did not take kindly to these "antisemites" in our midst, especially when the boiler went kaput and they demanded we pay to replace it. I couldn't understand how my parents could again make the same mistake—taking in Ms. Cowie when buying and taking in the Ukrainians when selling.

When our ride to the airport arrived, Ma and the Ukrainians were still fighting over who would pay for the boiler. Not wanting to miss our flight, Ma jumped into the car and we sped off. Within a minute or two, she screamed out, "Where's Rosalie?" We circled back. My five-year-old sister was standing at the curb sobbing, incredulous that we would leave without her. On the way to the airport, Ma gave us our marching orders: "If anyone asks you a question, always answer, 'I don't know.'"

Though my parents tried to imbue us with vigilance, they were easily bamboozled, even by their own kin. Before we left Cleveland, Pop's uncle wrote that he had an apartment for us on Serrano Avenue, and he requested two months' rent in advance. Our new home was a one-bedroom bungalow on the eastern side of Los Angeles, far from where most survivor families resided. Ma and Pop had to sleep in the living room on a bed that swung out of a closet. Children were not welcome in the complex. Pop's uncle made an exception for us. Not wanting to disturb the neighbors, Ma kept us inside when we were not at school. I still managed to kick a ball through one of the front-door windowpanes. Not sure if it was an accident.

I missed Mike Gordon, my abandoned comic book and baseball card collections, the Cleveland Indians, my half blue-half green bike, and nearby elementary school. Now I had to walk many blocks to get to school, including a long stretch over the Hollywood Freeway. Some paradise!

Rose and I now had a better grasp of what it meant to be "displaced persons." Yet we didn't complain. Our discomfort seemed trivial compared to what Ma and Pop had endured. We didn't need much. We had each other.

One day we received a visit from two Bedzin survivor friends, Sophie Hamburger and Hanka Appel. After surveying our living conditions, they promised to find us a bigger place in a better neighborhood for less rent. A couple months later we moved into a roomy two-bedroom apartment in a four-unit building on Wooster Street. Sophie's family lived in the adjacent building.

A family with a son my age named Zamir Tarmu soon moved in across the hall from us. He grew up in Ein Hod, an Israeli artists' colony. His mother, Galya, was an American painter and his stepfather, Yehuda, an Auschwitz survivor.

Their apartment always smelled of oil paint. The living room floor looked like a Jackson Pollock painting, not that I knew who Pollock was then. The walls displayed large canvases of Galya's work, often depicting naked people. I never missed a chance to catch a peak at the nudist magazines she kept on hand for anatomical reference.

The Bohemian lifestyle of the Tarmus enchanted me. My musical world expanded from Motown to Mozart and Monk. I encountered people who were nothing like our circle of survivors. The Tarmus' literati crowd included poet-activist Jack Hirschman and his wife, Ruth, a public radio pioneer.

When Zamir wasn't practicing his cello or guitar, he would come over and play board games and watch television with Rose and me. We never missed an episode of *The Twilight Zone*. Zamir and I rode our bikes together to Louis Pasteur Junior High and on the way home stopped at the post office to buy stamps for our collections. You might say we bonded over this hobby. "Do you collect stamps?" was the first thing I asked Zamir upon meeting him. During our Fairfax High days, he drove around in his red Austin Healy sports car. Zamir was handsome and he always had a cute girlfriend. He was cool. Turned me on to Bob Dylan and pot.

Moving to Wooster Street brought my parents back into the survivor sphere of mutual assistance. Pop got his first and only job in America thanks to the husband of one of Ma's Dabrowa friends who worked for Lear Avionics in Santa Monica. He put in a good word for Pop, who was a precision mechanic, a skill he had acquired in Bedzin and that helped keep him alive in Auschwitz. Pop's new job was short-lived. He was among the layoffs resulting from Lear's 1962 merger with the Siegler Corporation.

Ma found work as a seamstress for a company founded by Irene Lentz, the illustrious Hollywood fashion and costume designer. At Irene Inc., a 12,000-square-foot factory in Culver City, Ma sewed clothes for movie stars. She remembers sitting with Doris Day while putting the final touches on a costume for her 1961 film, *Lover Come Back*. This job too was short-lived. Ma could no longer stand to work under the shop's oppressive German foreman. She would come home from work complaining to Pop, "He wouldn't even let me go to the bathroom. It was like being in a concentration camp." Pop told her to quit and she did. She applied for a job as a saleswoman at a downtown clothing store owned by Holocaust survivors. When Ma entered for the first time, she spotted a twenty-dollar bill on the floor and immediately handed it to the owner. It was a test. Ma worked at Henry's Sweaterland for the next twenty-five years.

— *marty* —

Land of Palm Trees

In early 1965 my father lost his job, after having worked at a clothing store for many years. The news came as a shock. Not only were my father and the store owner close friends, but our families often got together socially. The cause of the layoff might have had something to do with his employer-friend remarrying after the death of his first wife. Whatever the reason, it must have been quite a blow for my father. Not only had he lost a source of income, I think he also felt somewhat betrayed by his friend.

My father decided to explore work possibilities in Los Angeles, where his brother Jack and a number of survivor friends lived. After several weeks away, during one of his regular phone calls home, he asked my mother to hand me the receiver. He said, "I want to move the family to California. But if you don't agree, I will come home and we'll stay in New York." At fifteen and a half, I felt settled in the Bronx, happy with my set of friends, and I was doing well in school. The thought of leaving behind everything familiar seemed more than I could bear. I told him, "I don't want you to do this." He asked me to think about it. I said that I would.

Within a short time, I overcame my initial resistance and began to get excited about leaving "the asphalt jungle" for the new frontier of the West. "How soon can we leave?" I asked my father. My friends were okay with this news, even expressing some jealousy that I was going off on this adventure to a place we had seen only on TV. Meanwhile, Aunt Aga and Uncle Lolek were already making plans to follow us to the City of Angels.

On Friday, July 2, 1965, after I completed my junior year of high school, my mother and I boarded an airplane for the first time. What I remember most vividly upon landing in Los Angeles were the palm trees towering over buildings against the backdrop of blue skies and the city's iconic hills. There didn't seem to be a building taller than a few stories. Not a fire escape in sight. Grass lined the streets. The most pleasant surprise of all was that our apartment on North Spaulding Avenue came with a large swimming pool.

I had to decide whether to attend summer school. In New York, summer school was for kids who had flunked a subject and needed to make up a class in order to progress to the next grade. Neither I nor any of my Bronx buddies had ever gone to summer school. After getting past the awkwardness of even mouthing "summer school," I took the advice of my parents' friends who promoted the idea of summer school at Fairfax High as a good way to make new friends. It was my introduction to California teenagers. They seemed more chill than my schoolmates at the Bronx High School of Science, where the focus was on academic excellence.

I didn't learn much in summer school and I made no friends. Worst of all, I missed out on going to the beach every day with my new best pal, Aron. Luckily, shortly after we met, Aron bought a blue 1960 Chevy Bel Air off a used car lot for $600 cash. Coming of age in LA meant getting your own car, and we were going to make the most of our newfound freedom.

— *aron* —

Elixir of Life

One word was taboo in our house: tuberculosis.

For much of my youth, I expected to die from TB or from some other ghastly disease. My tuberculin skin tests always came back positive. To my mind, the itchy red spot on my arm signaled imminent death. I'll never understand why my parents allowed doctors to continue testing me when they already knew that I'd been exposed to the bacteria at some point in my life.

My treatment as a lab rat continued in Los Angeles. I was offered up as a test subject in a UCLA study on the effects of a drug designed to prevent people with positive skin tests from ever getting TB. We never got the results. For all I know, they may have given me the placebo. The best thing about this experience was Pop treating me to a burger, fries, and Coke at a drugstore lunch counter near campus.

At some point, Ma and Pop got into the health food craze—whole grain breads, raw nuts, dried fruits, no preservatives. One of their prize possessions was a juicer. Every day after school, Rose and I were handed a tall glass of an orange-green liquid topped with a half-inch layer of foam. Eaten separately, carrots, grapes, celery, and green peppers posed no problem, but when blended together—disgusting!

Rose made a habit of secretly flushing her daily dose down the toilet of our shared bathroom. One day Ma caught Rose in the act. "You just committed an unforgivable sin," she scolded. "That was gold you just wasted. From now on you will drink your juice where I can watch you."

I literally held my nose when downing my parents' elixir of life, but one day I decided to make a quick getaway. I rushed out of the house, jumped into my car, and skidded out of the driveway onto the road. When I gazed into the rearview mirror, there was Ma chasing me down the middle of Spaulding Avenue holding up a glass full of that wretched juice.

So it went, until the day that Holocaust survivor and juice maven Nathan Langer appeared at our door carrying a wooden crate on his shoulder filled with bottles of fresh-squeezed apple juice. Ma knew Nathan's wife, Mira, from Dabrowa. Thereafter, Nathan and Mira would deliver a monthly supply of juice to help fortify Pop's health, never accepting payment. So ended the carrot-veggie juice era.

— *marty* —
Not the Bronx

When I began my senior year at Fairfax High, I realized how big a difference there was between the Bronx and Los Angeles public school systems. Having come from the Bronx High School of Science and having skipped the eighth grade, I had already completed most of the required classes to matriculate in California, making me eligible to graduate after only one semester.

I filled my schedule with electives that were not offered at my previous high school, like business machines, business law, and driver's ed. On my sixteenth birthday I got my driver's license—two years earlier than I would have been able to do so in New York.

I made the surprising discovery that I spoke English with an accent! I ordered "cawfee" cake at the school concession stand, just like a kid from the Bronx. The student server couldn't understand what I wanted. On the third go-around, she finally figured it out and handed me a slice. This happened again and again, making me feel like a foreigner. I soon mastered this new way of saying "cough-fee" but cringed each time at how unnatural it sounded.

I would visit the small clothing store that my father opened with a friend, Margo Rechnitz, who moved from New York to Los Angeles at about the same time we did. Many of their fellow survivors in the *shmata* (clothing or rag) business stepped up to help them get established.

The store was in Huntington Park, fourteen miles from our apartment, necessitating that my father learn to drive at the age of sixty-one. That's how we ended up with the white, four-door, 1960 Rambler Super with push-button gears. Having a car was a big step up from riding the D Train in New York, but these wheels were not on my short list of desirable cars. My father always took the surface street route to and from work, though the freeway would have been much faster. He would take the extra time without complaining. It must have been a giant leap for him just to get behind the wheel.

Being a pedestrian in Los Angeles required some adjustments as well. The first time I accompanied my father to his store, we were waiting at a crosswalk when he started walking and signaled for me to follow. I hesitated. As a street-smart kid who knew how to avoid being run down, I didn't quite trust my father's judgment that all was clear. I thought, "What's going on with my father! Doesn't he see the cars coming in our direction?" I didn't yet know that in this new land, vehicles actually stopped for pedestrians in a crosswalk.

One thing I knew for sure, this was not the Bronx!

— *aron* —

A Chat with Elvis

In our senior year, Marty and I were practically joined at the hip. On school nights we hung out in his bedroom, did our homework together, and watched TV, never missing an episode of *I Spy*. Marty's dad seemed to take great pleasure in bringing us a succession of snacks. Marty's mom stayed in the background, a loving presence.

Our high school buddies were all Jewish. On Saturday nights we cruised up and down Hollywood Boulevard hoping to pick up girls. We usually struck out, ending the night at Pink's Hot Dogs on North La Brea Avenue, gorging ourselves on foot-long franks slathered with chili and raw onions.

My love life was nothing to brag about. I was attracted to Pearl, a rather reserved girl my age who lived in the apartment next to ours on North Spaulding Avenue. She was the older daughter of a Jewish survivor family that had immigrated to the States from Poland in the late 1950s.

After spending a lot of time making small talk in her apartment, I asked Pearl out to a movie. Relishing my first chance to be alone with her in the dark, I leaned over to kiss her. She pushed me away. Though we thought of ourselves as boyfriend and girlfriend, our relationship went nowhere. After a few frustrating months, I ran into her lively best friend, Sue, at a party. We danced. I thought we kind of hit it off. The next day, Sue snitched on me. Pearl turned to ice. Sue started dating Marty, and I was left in the cold.

I turned my attention to a pretty Israeli girl in history class. When she told me about her love of classical music, I asked her on a date to attend a chamber music concert at the University of Southern California. To impress her, I tuned the car radio to a classical music station. I thought things had gone well, aside from my nodding off during the performance.

The next day at school, she fumed, "You lied to me. You aren't really into classical music. I'll never go out with you again!" I felt bad about not being honest with her, but I committed the same faux pas on a subsequent date.

"What do you think of folk singer Buffy Sainte-Marie?"

"Oh, I like him."

"But Buffy is a woman."

Silence.

Though I was open to classical and folk, my music of choice was rock 'n' roll, and the greatest thrill of my life was a personal encounter with Elvis Presley.

The story begins with my neighborhood paper route. After school and on weekend mornings a red truck would drop off stacks of newspapers at 920 North Spaulding Avenue. I would then trifold and rubber band each newspaper before loading them all in the canvas saddle bag straddling my bike. One day my boss told me that the person who covered the Samuel

Goldwyn Studio was quitting and offered me that job. I said yes and soon found myself on sound stages only steps away from Jack Lemmon, Kim Novak, Burt Lancaster, Frankie Avalon, and many other movie stars. I got my first close look at Hollywood royalty, admiring their fancy cars, like Samuel Goldwyn Jr.'s Jaguar XKE and composer Andre Previn's sporty Mercedes-Benz convertible.

One afternoon while hawking newspapers on set, Elvis Presley approached me and said, "Hi. What's your name?" "Aron," I replied. "That's my middle name," he said smiling. I thought, how amazing that "The King" would take notice of a lowly paperboy. Maybe it was because we had a similar hairstyle. I had the presence to ask for his autograph and handed him a slip of paper. He signed it and then asked one of his assistants to bring him a headshot, which he addressed "To Aron." Elvis was a real *mensch*!

I went on to become the busboy at the studio commissary. Enchanted by the show biz scene, I set my sights on someday becoming a movie producer.

— *marty* —
Like Brothers

Aron's roomy Chevy was our primary mode of transportation. We used my father's Rambler, the "uncoolest" car you could imagine, only as a last resort when riding together. We'd often go to Santa Monica beach, where I learned how to body surf, almost drowning once after being caught in the undertow.

Aron's sister, Rose, sometimes hung out with us in my parents' apartment. Just as Aron had already filled the vacancy of my not having a brother, Rose naturally slipped into the little sister role. I remember being struck by how gently and naturally my father related to her, allowing her to feel at ease in his presence.

Aron introduced me to a cute blonde girl named Sue. Though I was a senior and she a junior, Sue was actually a year older than me. We began dating during my last semester at Fairfax High. Her parents were also survivors. I soon discovered the recreational appeal of drive-in movie theaters, having the privacy of a car, darkness, and fogged up windows.

Whenever there was a vacant apartment in his parents' building, Aron was tasked with painting it. He once cajoled me into assisting him. This meant that there were two so-so painters on the job. We got paid and thought about taking on more jobs, but we could tell that this wasn't our strong suit.

Aron would occasionally take me along on his newspaper route inside the Samuel Goldwyn Studio. I got to visit sets of current TV shows like *The Fugitive* and *My Mother the Car*. This experience was about as far from the confines of the Bronx as one could get. I could see why Aron wanted to become a movie producer.

— *aron* —

An Unceremonious Ending

My classes at Fairfax High were uninspiring, except for biology. I spent many days hiking happily through the Hollywood hills gathering chaparral specimens for my class project. I also took a liking to the phrase, "ontogeny recapitulates phylogeny," meaning the development of the embryo follows the evolutionary history of the organism. I would quote it at every opportunity to impress girls with my sophisticated knowledge of science.

If I were asked to grade my high school, I'd give it a C for education and an A for entertainment. One of our guest concerts featured Fairfax alum Herb Alpert and his Tijuana Brass band. Another starred LA's own long-haired rockers, the Byrds, performing their hit songs, "Mr. Tambourine Man," "Turn! Turn! Turn!" and "Eight Miles High." Hearing these songs always transports me back to their concert in our high school auditorium.

My worst day of high school was the last. We seniors were not required to attend classes. I innocently wandered onto the athletic field, unaware that a special pass was required. A coach called me over and ordered me to bend forward and grab my ankles. He then pulled a wooden paddle from his pocket, walked behind me, and delivered a thunderous smack. During lunch break, a patrolling teacher overheard me telling my friends how that man "really kicked my ass." The teacher wrote me up for swearing and ordered me to proceed straight to the school office. The principal asked me why I used foul language on school grounds. "That's what actually happened to me earlier in the day," I explained, adding that I was an excellent student. With that, I pulled out my ace in the hole—a straight-A report card—and handed it to him. He looked it over and, nodding approvingly, shook my hand. Case closed.

Graduation was a non-event for both Marty and me. We didn't even bother to attend the ceremony. Caps and gowns were for squares. Our parents expected us to do well in school, but secular rites of passage were outside their lived experience. I don't think we even told them about the event, making it easier for us to quietly opt out.

Rituals and formal occasions have always made me feel uneasy, particularly when I am the center of attention. My preference to remain unnoticed in a crowd may be related to Ma's experience the first day in Grünberg concentration camp, when she was beaten for speaking out when the director cynically asked the new arrivals, "Who wants to go home?" The carefree days of high school had come to an end. Marty and I had both been accepted to UCLA. The next decade would forge us in ways we couldn't have imagined.

chapter three

Love and War

College, Israel, and Back

— *aron* —

The Big Leagues

During my freshman year, I was still sharing a bedroom with my sister at 920 North Spaulding. My plan was to move out in increments, starting with a bachelor apartment just up the street. To cover expenses, I tried different jobs.

I worked for one day at a textile factory in downtown LA owned by Jack Seidner, a survivor who was related to Ma. He did her a big favor hiring an inexperienced kid. On the first day, Jack stood me in front of a knitting contraption three times my height. I imagined Ma operating something like this in the Grünberg concentration camp. My job was simple, he said. "All you need to do is press this red button in case the machine malfunctions." He left me there alone. A few minutes later the contraption started to go haywire. I pressed the red button. It did nothing. I pressed it again and again. Nothing. The machine soon spun out of control. An alarm went off. Jack came running. Visibly upset, he blamed me for the "disaster." Clearly, I hadn't inherited the life-saving mechanical abilities of my parents.

I was better suited as a weekend shoe salesman at Leed's on the corner of Hollywood and Vine. One of the fringe benefits was meeting women.

One day a flirtatious customer told me she was a dancer at Whisky a Go Go, a popular Sunset Strip night club. "Want to watch me dance?" she whispered. How could I refuse? After work I drove her to the club. Along the way, we heard a radio announcement that Robert Kennedy had just been shot at the Ambassador Hotel in Los Angeles by a Palestinian. My date blurted out, "Oh, the Jews are the cause of all the world's problems." Her words shocked me into silence. I had not yet found my Jewish voice.

My freshman year at UCLA was intimidating. It was the big leagues. I looked with awe at older students strutting around campus. Marty and I both failed the mandatory writing readiness test and were consigned to the "Dummy English" class.

The first day of Economics 101 was another wake-up call. Seeing graphs and formulas spread across the blackboard reminded me of how much I dreaded math. It dawned on me that choosing Business Administration as my major was as preposterous as my hope of ever becoming a movie producer.

Marty and I took many of the same courses after we changed our major to psychology. Our favorite course was taught by Dr. Carl Faber. His reading list included Hermann Hess's *Siddhartha*, Nikos Kazantzakis's *Zorba the Greek*, and J. D. Salinger's *Franny and Zooey*. No tests. The only requirement was a personal essay on self-discovery. Dr. Faber wanted to empower us students to self-actualize by becoming the authors of our own life stories.

We were uninspired by our other psych professors. One of them was so predictable that we could purchase transcripts of his lectures on the black market along with three variations of his multiple-choice final exam.

Not being into basketball, I missed the chance to see the great Lew Alcindor (Kareem Abdul-Jabbar) play at UCLA's Pauley Pavilion. I did take advantage of music performances by pop and jazz groups like Linda Ronstadt and the Stone Poneys, The Association, and The Cannonball Adderley Quintet. By then I was also into jazz.

My weekends became routine. Friday night Shabbat dinner with my parents and sister; Saturdays at Leeds Shoes; Saturday nights with my girlfriend, a nice Jewish girl who always waited for me to open the car door for her; and Sundays working as a bookkeeper in the back office of Robaire's, a French restaurant in the Valley.

All that was about to change as reverberations of world events began to shake up our narrowly focused outlooks.

Psych 101

I entered UCLA in January 1966 at the tender age of sixteen. Aron was already eighteen. We selected business as our major, likely because we didn't have a clue as to what we really wanted to study.

In the mandatory English class, I chose to write a short essay on love. One day the instructor read an anonymous sampling of some of our writings, using the opportunity to point out what worked and what didn't. The pride I felt at having my paper selected quickly evaporated when he used it as an example of a topic that was way too broad for the assignment.

That first semester we both took Physical Anthropology 101, taught by an icon in the field, Dr. Joseph Birdsell. His teaching assistant, a cool guy named Mike West, always wore a blue chambray work shirt, off-white jeans, and tan desert boots. Aron and I liked this outfit so much that we adopted his look. A short-sleeved blue shirt and sandals was the summer uniform version.

For the fall 1966 semester, we both enrolled in Dr. Carl Faber's class. It was there that we immersed ourselves more deeply in the field of psychology. Faber, a devotee of the Swiss psychiatrist Carl Jung, had a gift for conveying his passion for authentic human interactions that went beyond academics.

After taking Dr. Faber's class, Aron and I officially changed our majors to psychology.

In early 1967, Aron and I rented a one-bedroom apartment on Formosa Avenue about a mile east of North Spaulding. Aron got the bedroom. I slept in the living room on the Murphy Bed that opened from the wall. Rent was $125/month—pretty reasonable—but the apartment was not without some hassles. After being woken up several times a night to people knocking on our neighbor's door, we gathered that her steady stream of male visitors weren't friends so much as clients.

Aron, Dave Silber (a son of survivors who lived upstairs from Aron's family at 920 North Spaulding), and I worked weekends as shoe salesmen. Though the store catered to women, some of our customers were men who leaned toward high-heeled pumps dyed in flashy colors. We made decent money and met a lot of girls. Working alongside older guys who did this as a career, we were required to wear suits and ties. One day I showed up for work unshaven. Our boss, Mr. Wall, sent me off to get shaved. It was the first time I had a shave by a barber with a straight razor, and I liked it.

I saved up $550 to buy my first car, a 1962 Karmann Ghia convertible. At that time, I didn't feel any compunction about owning a German car. I had never driven a stick shift, and this one, I quickly discovered, had a faulty clutch. It stalled many times before I finally got it home. Despite the mechanical challenges that this car presented, I loved it! It was then, as it would likely be today, a really cool car. Once I got the clutch repaired, it drove wonderfully. I typically kept the top down, unless it was raining, which in Southern California was basically never.

During spring break in 1967, Aron and I piled into Zamir Tarmu's van, along with members of his band, and headed to Ensenada, Mexico. Just as we crossed the border into Mexico, a US Border Patrol officer pulled us over to check everyone's ID. I was the only one under eighteen. Minors unaccompanied by a parent were prohibited from entering Mexico. He ordered me to step out of the vehicle and go home. I walked back across the border and waited for a while before making a second attempt on foot. I rejoined our group and for the next three days was an outlaw in Mexico.

Feeling awkward about being a younger kid in college, I began seeing a counselor at UCLA's Student Health Center, Dr. Paul Philippe, recommended by Dr. Faber. He was extraordinarily helpful in boosting my self-confidence. I may have reminded him of himself some twenty years earlier. He was French, very cool, drove an old Porsche, and introduced me to the book *In Praise of Older Women*. At his recommendation I participated in one of UCLA's weekend colloquium programs held in the San Bernardino Mountains.

The first event I attended, "On the Nature of Love," marked the beginning of my transformation from being just another college kid to being part of a community of seekers. I danced freely, expressed myself, and experienced being seen and heard. It was like being launched into a new realm. I became involved with a new circle of friends and faculty that didn't include Aron. There wasn't any animosity between us. It was just the natural result of getting older and broadening my interests. I moved into a small apartment in Venice Beach with Tom, whom I had met at one of the colloquia. Dr. Faber hired me as a reader to assist in grading hundreds of term papers and projects. Around this time I found myself becoming increasingly aware of what was happening in the world and became active in the anti-Vietnam War and Black Power movements on campus.

— *aron* —

The Awakening

From my perspective, Marty had replaced me with his new buddy, Tom. It bothered me, but I understood his need to break out of our bubble. My primary concern was grades. It was literally a matter of life and death. Any male student whose GPA fell below a certain threshold risked losing his student deferment and ending up in Vietnam. From 1966 through 1970, more than a million men were inducted into the US armed forces.

The UCLA campus was a hive of political activity. Men were burning their draft cards. Women were burning their bras. I witnessed one anti-war protester burn his own arm with Napalm, the incendiary gel that American planes were dropping on people in North Vietnam. I felt solidarity with these activists but couldn't see myself on the barricades of any political struggle. I was too self-involved, too focused on my schoolwork and social life.

That all changed late one night in my sophomore year. While studying for final exams, I took a break and turned on the radio. The program was interrupted by an announcement that Israel was at war with several Arab nations. The news came as a total shock. I had no idea about the growing tensions that had led up to the June 1967 war. The specter of another Holocaust shook me to the core. I began to tremble uncontrollably, vowing that if Israel survived, I would never again sit on the sidelines of Jewish history.

The next morning I told Zamir of my pledge. It so happened that a close friend of his family, Naomi Gan, was the cultural attaché at the Israeli consulate in Los Angeles. She informed us that Tel Aviv University was recruiting American students for its first ever junior year abroad study program.

— *marty* —
Going to Israel

When the June 1967 war broke out, I don't remember being overly concerned. I wasn't particularly attuned to what was happening in the Middle East. My focus was on other issues, such as Vietnam and civil rights. But by the spring of 1968, feeling overwhelmed by all the political turbulence on campus, I was ready for a change.

I applied to a UCLA-University of Madrid student exchange program. Having studied Spanish, I thought Madrid was as good a place as any to get away, but my application was rejected. Around that same time, Aron told me about a new junior year program for American students at the University of Tel Aviv. I jumped at the opportunity. We met with Zamir's friend at the Israeli consulate. She pulled a few strings, and we got into the program on full scholarships.

Aron and I were back on the same track again.

When I shared my plans with some of my friends, they thought it was cool but didn't quite grasp the significance of Israel to me. A few other friends who were Black and planning to travel to Africa immediately got it.

I had always felt a special connection to Israel through my parents, who had considered settling in Palestine after their liberation. My father's nephew, Zvi, immigrated there after the war. His family lived in Kfar Saba, near Tel Aviv. Mom had a niece on a kibbutz in the Beit Shean Valley. My parents could take solace in knowing that I'd be welcomed by our family members in Israel. Perhaps my move vicariously fulfilled the yearning they had felt to be in the Jewish homeland while trapped in Nazi-occupied Europe during the war.

In mid-June, after completing my spring semester at UCLA, I traveled alone from LA to New York, then on to Luxembourg. I then took a train to Rome and spent a few wonderful days exploring the city before making my way to a remote airfield at 2:00 in the morning, where a chartered plane stood waiting alongside a small group of American students.

At Israel's Lod Airport, we were greeted by representatives of the program, who directed us to a waiting bus outside the terminal. Before hopping aboard, I looked up at Israel's waving blue and white flag, a symbol of triumph over the forces bent on our people's destruction through the ages. I had never felt so awestruck. Throughout my time in Israel, when seeing the flag, I would often pause in silence and take in the marvel of an independent Jewish state.

Since dormitory accommodations had not yet been completed, our group was housed off-campus in a lovely row of villas in the beach-side community of Herzliya Pituah. The whole setup was pretty cushy. I had two roommates, one of whom had also lived in Venice, California. Each morning we would be transported to the Tel Aviv University campus in the back of trucks with bench seats (a common mode of transport back then) for *ulpan,* a Hebrew prep course. Other than that, we were pretty much free to do as we pleased.

On the second day, I made my way by bus to Kfar Saba to meet my cousin Zvi and his family. It would be an understatement to say that they welcomed me like royalty. Zvi had last seen my father twenty-five years earlier in Bedzin, after Jerry literally pulled him from a transport truck bound for Auschwitz. Zvi made no secret of his love and adoration for my father. I was always being offered first dibs on everything in their tiny apartment, including use of the shower. This was no small thing, as a limited amount of hot water was produced by the solar "boiler" on their roof.

During my visits to their home, I would often sit in their kitchen while Miriam, Zvi's wife, who was born in Jerusalem to a Sephardic Jewish family, baked tasty goodies. She would patiently tell me stories in basic Hebrew about the early days after Israel's independence and about the larger-than-life heroes of that time. As my Hebrew became more proficient, so did my understanding of this period in Israeli history.

With my cousin and his family to lean on, I became more and more in tune with the land and the people. I realized that becoming Israeli wasn't like turning on a switch; it would take considerable time, effort, and commitment.

— *aron* —

VIP Treatment

With the Tel Aviv university dorms still under construction, our group of about fifty students were housed in an upscale seaside town north of the city. I shared a room with three other students in a villa where Cuban diplomats had resided before Fidel Castro severed ties with Israel in the wake of the Six-Day War.

As the first group of American students to study at Tel Aviv University, we received VIP treatment. The news media took an interest in us. We met with the who's who of Israel. The future prime minister, Golda Meir, came to greet us. We traveled to Kibbutz Sde Boker in the Negev Desert, where the nation's founding prime minister, David Ben-Gurion, inspired us with stories about how the early Zionist pioneers had made the desert bloom. To orient us to Israel's social and political landscape, the program organizers arranged for a series of guest lectures by leading Israeli historians, generals, and diplomats. We also spent an afternoon hearing from Anwar Nuseibah, Jordan's former minister of defense, who presented an Arab perspective on current events.

Israel's decisive military victory in the 1967 Six-Day War opened geographic areas that had been off-limits to Jews. We prayed at the Western

Wall in Jerusalem, snorkeled in the Red Sea, rode camels in the Sinai, and skied on the slopes of Mt. Hermon.

After completing a basic Hebrew *ulpan* class, our group spent a week volunteering at various kibbutzim. Dave Silber and I were assigned to Kibbutz Hulata in the north, neighboring a nature preserve. On our first morning, Dave and I were delivered by tractor to the kibbutz chicken coop, where we spent the day shoveling poop into wheelbarrows that were dumped into the fishpond as feed. We were happy to get back to the villas.

Our group studied with visiting professors from Cornell, MIT, NYU, and other top American universities. They challenged me intellectually as never before, underscoring the qualitative difference between so-so and superlative higher education.

By year's end, I was infatuated with Israel. I felt at home and liberated in our ancestral homeland. At night I would sometimes walk to the beach and imagine myself as Zorba the Greek dancing with the waves. Dr. Faber would have been proud.

In letters to my parents, I shared many of my experiences in Israel, leaving out one ironic detail. At the very moment of my re-embrace of Jewish life, I fell in love with a woman of Polish-Catholic descent. I also made no mention of my decision to make Israel my home after graduating from UCLA.

Turning Point

I stuck with the Tel Aviv University program that summer, focusing on mastering Hebrew. Everyone in the program was assigned a week-long stint on a pre-approved kibbutz. The Israeli frontier was calling. Another buddy in the program and I went off on our own. We traveled north by bus until we reached Tiberias, a town on the banks of the Sea of Galilee. From there we hitchhiked to Kibbutz Mevo Hama, a newly established settlement on the Golan Heights near the border with Syria.

I don't recall any "elders" on the kibbutz; everyone was in their twenties and thirties. Hot water was not available. To bathe we had to travel to a neighboring kibbutz. Each morning we and a group of kibbutz members, some armed with Uzi submachine guns, would be transported by truck to some cotton fields. There we were handed a large sack into which we deposited the cotton we handpicked under the hot sun. On some mornings we couldn't ride to the fields because an army patrol had discovered landmines planted along the road by infiltrators from Syria. It was just part of daily life on the frontier.

There was a rugged beauty and vastness to the Golan Heights, which had been the border with Syria until the Six-Day War. Syrian artillery used to randomly shell Israeli settlements along the shore of the Sea of Galilee. From a purely strategic and security perspective, Israel's capture and annexation of this territory seemed to be very logical (though not for Syria of course).

After spending a couple of weeks on Kibbutz Mevo Hama, I made my way to Jerusalem. I had by then decided not to return to the Tel Aviv University program because it was apparent to me that our group would go on living comfortably outside the lifestyles of most Israelis. Not what I had signed on for.

In Jerusalem I moved from place to place, even being a "squatter" at times. I was successful in my effort to transfer to Hebrew University and moved in with two Israelis and a Canadian who spoke impeccable Hebrew. In our small, two-bedroom flat, I was able to immerse myself in the Hebrew language as never before. I even began dreaming in Hebrew, though I didn't always understand what was being said. I took this as a sign that I was making progress in my quest to master the language.

In the spring of 1969, two Hebrew University students were killed in a bombing of a supermarket near where I shopped. The following afternoon a memorial service was held on campus to commemorate their lives and to protest terrorism. This was the first student demonstration I had participated in since my UCLA days. Several hundred people were present, including the mother of one of the victims. I found myself standing next to her. She was weeping inconsolably. Witnessing the torment of a parent grieving for a murdered child pained me deeply. Only later would I gain insight into my intense reaction.

What I experienced at that moment reinforced my decision to move permanently to Israel and defend the Jewish state. I was unwilling to be a bystander, to witness such atrocities and not take action to prevent them. After completing my undergraduate degree at UCLA, I would return to Israel and become a soldier in a Jewish army to defend our people's historic homeland.

— *aron* —

Merilyn

Merilyn Malek had signed up for the Tel Aviv University program, though she had no personal ties to the Jewish people. Despite growing up in politically conservative Anaheim, California, home of Disneyland, Merilyn had a rebellious streak. Before going to Israel, she was dating a member of the Black Panthers.

Having only just met her, I was surprised when Merilyn accepted my invitation to spend a weekend hitchhiking together up the Mediterranean coast. We slept on beaches along the way and visited Ein Hod, the hilltop artist's village where Zamir had lived as a young child. We spent the night on the rooftop of a stone building beneath a starry sky.

During spring break we traveled to Greece and visited the former home of Nikos Kazantzakis, author of *Zorba the Greek*, in the city of Heraklion on the island of Crete. We then followed the footsteps of Joni Mitchell, Bob Dylan, and Joan Baez to "the hippie caves of Matala." For the next few days, we camped in a cave overlooking a scenic cove.

On the second night, we decided to treat ourselves to a dinner of escargot. We gathered about a dozen or so jumbo snails in the wild. As a precautionary measure, I showed the snails to the clerk of the seaside convenience store and pointed to my mouth. He nodded approvingly. Back in the cave, we heated a can of tomato sauce over a wood fire and stirred in our slithery catch of the day. In the middle of the night, I awoke with a bad case of the runs. No toilets. Only one designated cave for all. Not the adventure I'd anticipated.

The following morning I confronted the clerk, "You said we could eat the snails." He shrugged and said, "You must give them time to digest their food." Now he tells me! I purchased a bottle of Pepto Bismol. He had a ready supply.

— *marty* —

Returning Home

After completing my year at Hebrew University, I prepared a backpack and set out on a hike through western Europe. My father suggested that I stop in Hamburg, Germany, to visit his cousins, Helen and Izek, and ask them to help me purchase a Volkswagen that could be shipped to Los Angeles. By this time I had decided that I didn't want a German-made car in the family. It just didn't feel right. I wanted as little to do with Germany as possible. How interesting, I thought, that my father did not share my sentiments about boycotting German products. He let it go, and we didn't discuss it again.

I flew to Athens and stayed with some friends who had participated in the Tel Aviv University program. After a few days of roaming around the Greek capital, I boarded a boat bound for an overnight journey to Crete. I ordered a cup of Turkish coffee, momentarily forgetting about the animosity between Greeks and Turks. My faux pas was met with amusement by the other passengers. Lucky for me, no ultra-nationalist Greek was within earshot.

From the port city of Heraklion, I headed by bus to the hippie caves in Matala, stopping along the way at the ancient Minoan ruins of Knossos. I was taken aback to learn that every cave was occupied. The area's only hotel had no vacancy. Fortunately, two Greek guys who grasped my predicament invited me to share their room, providing a bed and good company. After a week on Crete, I boarded a boat back to Athens, and this time ordered coffee more thoughtfully.

Schlepping around Europe soon lost its allure. I didn't want to be just another tourist. I took a train to Brussels, where I boarded a plane back to the US. My homecoming coincided with the first human landing on the moon. The airwaves abounded with Astronaut Neil Armstrong's famous line: "One small step for man, one giant leap for mankind." I was making my first step back into the familiar and comfortable world of Los Angeles, determined not to make it a step backwards.

— *aron* —

The Purloined Letter

Rose and I agreed that it would be best to wait until I returned to Los Angeles before telling Ma and Pop about Merilyn. Ma must have sensed that I was hiding something when she couldn't restrain herself from opening one of my letters addressed to Rose. Discovering that I was in a relationship with a gentile girl was her worst nightmare come true, a catastrophe. "That night," Ma later told me, "I had to tie a belt around my knees to keep them from knocking together."

On all future letters home, I would write, "HAND OVER TO ROSE!"

Rose alone was privy to my audacious adventures in Israel, like the time Merilyn and I were caught spending the night together in the dormitory of a yeshiva in Jerusalem where a couple of guys who had dropped out of the Tel Aviv University program were studying.

"You should have seen the rabbi's face when he walked in the next morning," I wrote to Rose. "He refused to believe that Merilyn was not Jewish and made us both go into the sanctuary to pray for our sins. As atonement, I had to wear *tefillin*, phylacteries, on my forehead and left arm while holding a Torah scroll."

After our year in Israel, Merilyn and I returned to UCLA to complete our studies in psychology. We rented a small apartment in Venice Beach. It was my hope that after meeting Merilyn, Ma would come to accept her. Dream on. While visiting my parents on one occasion, Ma and Merilyn got into a tiff. It began when Ma insisted on combing my hair. I don't know what possessed her. Perhaps she was asserting her maternal right to groom her son. I would have none of it and demanded that she stop. She wouldn't.

At that point, Merilyn lost her cool and yelled, "Leave him alone!" Ma's eyes widened with indignation but said not another word. On our drive home, I commented to Merilyn, "Now that's just the kind of thing my mother will forgive but never forget."

There were no more flare-ups, but tensions simmered. Then one day, Ma's friend Hanka Leiber took her to see a movie. They drove up to Hollywood Boulevard and watched Franco Zeffirelli's adaptation of Shakespeare's *Romeo and Juliet*. The message of this tragic tale—the death of two young lovers resulting from parental prejudice and intergroup hatred—was not lost on Ma. Never again did she interfere in my relationship with Merilyn. The stakes were just too high!

Merilyn and I agreed that after we completed our undergraduate studies, we would both make *aliyah*, immigrate to Israel. She began a conversion to Judaism program with UCLA's Hillel director, Rabbi Richard Levy. Everything was on track.

— *marty* —

Boy, Were We Arrogant!

When Aron and I returned from Israel, one of our first stops was to visit Dr. Faber. He listened with great interest to our stories about how our year there had transformed us into lovers of Zion and he asked us to be guest speakers at his popular extension class. We said yes, though neither of us had ever done any public speaking.

The event was billed as "Two Controversial Speakers on the Middle East." We found this framing somewhat curious. In our minds, we were simply two seekers who had found our Israel experience profoundly liberating.

The large auditorium was packed. In addition to Dr. Faber's students, the audience included members of the press, an informant from the Anti-Defamation League (to the ADL, combining "controversial" and "Middle East" signaled Arabs), and a scattering of Jewish campus activists from across the political spectrum.

Turns out that Dr. Faber got it right. Controversial was an understatement. Our Zionist message caused a furor. We learned the hard way that American Jews did not want to be lectured about how they are afflicted with a "diaspora mentality" and that only in Israel can they live a dignified Jewish life. Standing on that stage, our only consolations were the sympathetic comments of some Christians in the audience.

Boy, were we arrogant!

— *aron* —

Out of My Shell

As one who shunned the limelight, putting myself out there in front of so many people in Dr. Faber's class was unnerving. The fury we unleashed among many of the Jews in the audience brought to mind what Ma had taught us as children: "Don't talk to strangers."

Not every Jew in attendance wanted to tar and feather us. Jewish campus activists in the crowd applauded our audacity. The designated Anti-Defamation League informant, Alain Rogier, introduced himself to me after the presentation with a broad smile and handshake. Mark Friedman, publisher of the campus Jewish newspaper, *Ha'am*, offered me a column, which I agreed to write even though I was a complete novice. My first piece, a review of Philip Roth's novel about a self-hating Jew, *Portnoy's Complaint*, jump-started my career as a journalist. Members of the Jewish Radical Community invited Merilyn and me to participate in their weekly Shabbat gatherings, opening the door to a new chapter in my life.

That evening, I came out of my shell.

— *marty* —

Gutcha, Lusha, and Ruthie

My family rarely sat down together for meals. I preferred eating in front of the TV. One evening my parents asked that we have dinner together in the dining room. I knew something was up.

— aron —

Aron's mother, Adela Kestenberg, wearing Nazi mandated Jewish armband, Dabrowa Gornicza, Poland, 1941

Aron's father, Wolf Manheimer, with Abram, his only surviving sibling, Paris, 1945

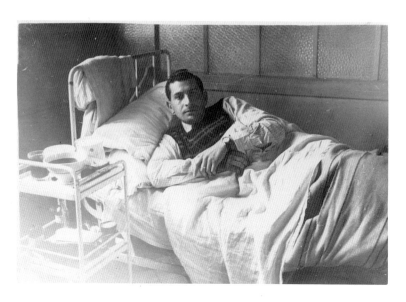

Wolf in tuberculosis sanatorium, Gauting, Germany, 1945

Adela and Wolf, wedding day,
Feldafing Displaced Persons Camp, Germany, 1947

Aron at age two, Munich, Germany, 1950

Aron's cousin Simon ("Shimonele"),
murdered in Auschwitz-Birkenau at age two, 1943

Aron's paternal grandfather, Aron Chaim Manheimer, murdered in Auschwitz-Birkenau, 1943

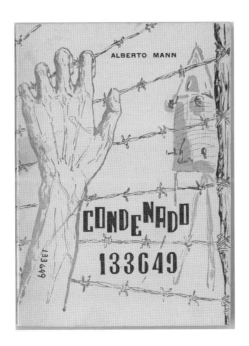

Cover of Abram's memoir, published under the pseudonym
Alberto Mann, Buenos Aires, Argentina, 1961

Aron's father's brother Heniek and his fiancée, Kadja Mandal.
Their fate is unknown.

Aron with sister, Rosalie (Rose), Cleveland, Ohio, 1959

Judy Hirt, Aron's *bashert* (destined soulmate), Jerusalem, 1972

Aron amidst tombstones, old Jewish cemetery, Bedzin, Poland, 1994

Aron with his son Noah, Auschwitz-Birkenau, 2004

Adela (*front, left center*) reunited with death march survivors, Volary, Czech Republic, 1995

Family reunion celebrating Adela's 100th birthday, Encino, California, 2020

— *marty* —

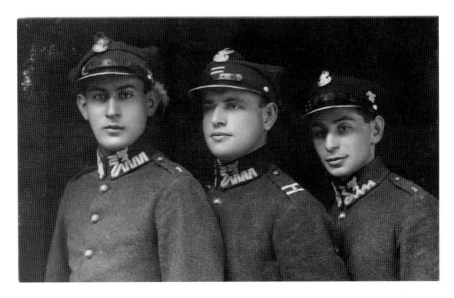

Marty's father, Jerry (*center*), in the Polish Army, circa 1925

Jerry courting Gutcha, circa 1930

Uncle Lolek (*left*) with his brother and a cousin, one shot and killed by Nazis in Poland, the other in Paris, circa 1935

Jerry with his first wife, Gutcha, and daughters, Ruthie (*left*) and Lusha, circa 1943

Jerry showing Auschwitz prisoner tattoo, circa 1945

Marty's mother, Sophie (*left*), and aunt Aga,
Feldafing Displaced Persons Camp, Germany, circa 1946

Marty in Captain Hook costume made by his mother, circa 1955

Marty at his bar mitzvah with his father (*standing right*), mother, Sophie (*sitting*), Aunt Aga, and Uncle Lolek (*standing left*), 1962

Marty during IDF officer training course, 1971

Marty and Marti's wedding, 1984

Marty (*left*) with Aron, Los Angeles, 2018. Photo by Rose Eichenbaum.

At the table, my father announced that he and my mother had something to tell me. He then said straight out that he had been married before the war. He had a wife named Gutcha and two daughters, Lusha and Ruthie. They had gone into hiding after the liquidation of the Bedzin ghetto. One day he went out looking for food. When he came back, his family was gone. They had been discovered by the Nazis and sent to their deaths in Auschwitz.

My father held his emotions in check, probably because he didn't want to upset me, or perhaps he had learned how to avoid tapping into that abyss. Those are all the details he shared. I immediately understood what Aunt Bronka and Cousin Helen had alluded to and so quickly dropped. I didn't ask for more details, though I did tell my father that I had heard some references to this story and had chosen not to pursue the matter before he was ready to tell me about it himself.

I didn't share that I had been trying to spare him the pain of revisiting his terrible loss and causing him excess worry about how the revelation might affect me. I had always found this history too traumatizing to want to know more. We never talked about it again. Years later, Aunt Aga told me that at the time of their deaths, Lusha was eleven and Ruthie, two and a half.

I now understood why my father had been so drawn to Aron's sister. When we became friends, Rose was Lusha's age at her death and even resembled her. My father acted toward Rose as if he knew how to connect with an eleven-year-old girl, and Aron's shy sister responded with uncharacteristic ease when he beckoned her with offerings of sliced apples or a piece of cake. He evidently chose to be gracious and "father-like" to Rose rather than to regard her as a sad reminder of his terrible loss.

— *aron* —

Jewish Radical Community

Every Shabbat, Merilyn and I would participate in a song-filled creative service with a dozen or so of our new Jewish Radical Community (JRC) friends in people's apartments. No one said a thing when a male member came in wearing a dress. JRC represented a wide range of Jewish ideologies from Socialist Zionists to anti-Zionist Bundists. Some were atheists, others believers. Some were gay, some straight. We took on many issues, from support of Soviet Jewry to the creation of university Jewish studies programs.

When Rose came to her first JRC Shabbat, Betzalel "Bitzy" Eichenbaum asked her, "How long have you been Aron's sister?" "Sixteen years," she replied. He decided to wait a few months before making his move. Bitzy rode around in a souped-up Honda 450. His motorcycle helmet had decals of the Israeli flag on one side and the Viet Cong flag on the other—red meat for the California Highway Patrol. More often than not, Bitzy could outrace and outmaneuver his uniformed pursuers.

Ma and Pop knew nothing about our involvement in JRC. I once joined a protest rally outside of a Jewish-owned business that allegedly was exploiting its employees. Ma worked about a block away at Henry's Sweaterland. I was less concerned about the police filming us, which they did, than Ma spotting her son passing out leaflets and my having to explain why I was engaging in class struggle when I should be in class.

One Passover, JRC planned a seder in rural California. We gathered at a grocery store parking lot on Goshen Street in West Los Angeles. Why there? Because the Torah mentions "The Land of Goshen" in connection with the Exodus. The leaflet announcing the event read: "Let Our People Go," referring to the plight of Soviet Jewry. The symbolic itinerary—"Starting in the Egyptian ghetto of Goshen . . . Stopping at the Red Sea . . . Ending in the Wilderness"—brought home the concept that we ourselves were once slaves in Egypt. Roasting a whole lamb over a fire pit for the seder meal seemed like a good idea at the time. Very biblical.

California Governor Ronald Reagan was our Pharaoh. He stood solidly behind the violent actions of the Los Angeles police on May 5, 1970, when they swarmed the UCLA campus in response to anti-war protests. From the roof of a building where Bitzy and I took refuge, we witnessed cops indiscriminately chase down and beat every student in sight. Police helicopters whirred above us. What were we thinking? Only a day earlier,

Ohio National Guardsmen had shot and killed four unarmed Kent State students and wounded nine.

— *marty* —
The Unspeakable

One afternoon while my father was at work, my mother took the unusual step of asking me to sit down to talk. "When you were away in Israel," she told me, "your father had a cancerous kidney removed." She cautioned me not to say anything about this to my father because no one had revealed to him the details of his illness.

I contacted several radiologists and found one in Beverly Hills who agreed to have a look at his X-rays. The doctor sat down with me and very empathetically described how there was a predictable progression of the disease, likely spreading to other parts of his body, ultimately resulting in death. On a more encouraging note, he pointed out that the most recent X-ray showed a remission of the disease. It seemed that for the time being the cancer had "disappeared." I was able to share what I had learned with my mother, Aunt Aga, and Uncle Lolek, but not with my father. He had never been told in a straightforward way that he had cancer. His kidney removal was described as "a surgical procedure." I suspect my father knew the truth all along but did not let on.

— *aron* —
My Indomitable Can-Do Spirit

With a new community of like-minded Jewish friends, my own newspaper column, and a steady girlfriend, my self-confidence was at an all-time high. That may explain why I saw fit to apply for a Rhodes Scholarship.

My face-to-face interview with a UCLA professor who screened candidates didn't go as well as I had expected.

"What is your sport?"

"Body surfing. Um . . . Ping Pong?"

"What is your main area of interest?"

"The Holocaust."

"Did you read *The Rise and Fall of the Third Reich?*"

"Yes." (I lied.)

"Do you agree with William Shirer's thesis in the book?"

"Um . . . I'll have to give that some thought."

Okay. So I was not Rhodes Scholar material. But I didn't allow that embarrassing encounter to shake my self-confidence. My biggest test was about to come.

The Jewish Radical Community opposed a plan announced by the Jewish Federation of Los Angeles in 1970 to fund another Jewish student facility at UCLA. We already had two: Hillel and Chabad House. What was needed were more Jewish student activities and programs. JRC won that battle. The Federation allocated funding for ten Jewish projects that would be administered by Hillel. My proposal for the creation of a West Coast Jewish quarterly was approved, though I hadn't a clue about how to actually produce a magazine. I sought the assistance of the Hillel director, Rabbi Richard Levy. Luckily, he had once been managing editor of the *Harvard Crimson* and offered to walk me through the process.

After I collected the articles for the first edition, I asked him, "What do I need to do next?"

"You need to create galleys."

"What's a galley?"

"It's a column of type that needs to be pasted onto forms. Decide on the size of the magazine, find a typesetter, and then come back prepared to paste it up."

A couple of weeks later, I arrived at the rabbi's house with the galleys, paste-up forms, photos, drawings, glue, and an assortment of cutting and measuring tools. Thus was the first edition of *Davka* (connoting "defiance") born on Rabbi Levy's dining room table.

The magazine's nine-member editorial review board consisted of Rabbi Levy, Merilyn Malek (my girlfriend), Alain Rogier (the guy ADL had sent to spy on "two controversial speakers on the Middle East"), Jon Kellerman (the future best-selling mystery writer), and three JRC friends.

I spent every free minute at the UCLA Hillel House working on the quarterly. The first edition appeared in November 1970. Its theme was "The Ills of American Jewry," and it opened with my editor's note:

> World Jewry is still convalescing from the tragedy that befell it during World War II. The survivors pictured here [a mother holding an American flag and her two small children] are among those that looked toward the United States for salvation and tried to forget the barbarism inflicted upon them and their people in Europe. But forgetting is impossible. The anxiety characteristic of an oppressed minority is omnipresent. We may try to forget that we are Jews. But what if we are suddenly reminded? On the other hand, we may assert our Jewishness. But what if we are ridiculed and humiliated as a result?
>
> The children pictured here probably have been and continue to be affected by the contradictions and tribulations of Jews living in *galut*, the diaspora. These children must have wondered or asked, "Why must we be different from everyone else?"
>
> Perhaps they have found Judaism relevant and beautiful in their lives. It is more probable that they feel indifferent to their Jewishness. Most depressingly, they may be wearing El Fatah [Palestinian National Liberation Movement] buttons at this moment.

My office mate at Hillel was Allan Wiesblott, who would later change his name to Noah benShea. He published one of his first poems, "screams," in the first edition of *Davka*. Three years later he would be the best man at our wedding. Today he is best known as the author of the international best-selling book, *Jacob the Baker*, which has been made into a feature film.

The fourth edition of *Davka* (Summer, 1971) was devoted to "The Jewish Woman," at the time a non-existent topic in Jewish journalism. My editor's note began: "Jewish womanhood is problematic for observant and non-observant Jews.... The Jewish woman is often confronted with stereotypes which insult and degrade her."

Rachel Adler wrote the lead story, "The Jew Who Wasn't There."

She concluded with a call to action: "For too many centuries, the Jewish woman has been a golem created by Jewish society. She cooked and bore and did her master's will, and when her tasks were done, the Divine Name was removed from her mouth. It is time for the golem to demand a soul."

Rachel Adler would become a pioneering feminist theologian, rabbi, and professor. In an interview marking her retirement from the Hebrew Union College in 2020, she was asked what the impetus was for her work. She replied:

> I cannot claim to have embarked on this project knowing where it would take me. Aron Hirt-Mannheimer ... who was then editing a small West Coast Jewish magazine called *Davka* ... proposed to publish an issue devoted to Jewish women and asked me to write. I piled the dining room table with my then-husband's [Orthodox Rabbi Moshe Adler] volumes of Talmud and Codes. All my questions and concerns poured out. After I gave Aron the result, it hit me that I had said some very subversive things, and I asked Aron to return this article, "The Jew Who Wasn't There," so I could destroy it. He refused. The issue sold out and had to be reprinted. Suddenly women's groups far from Los Angeles were discussing my article, and every rabbi I encountered was scolding me. Oddly, instead of making me remorseful, that convinced me that what I had said was true, and that I was never going to chicken out again.

Davka's Jewish Woman edition included a tribute to the heroism of the Jewish poet and anti-Nazi resistance fighter Hannah Senesch. The cover photo depicted three young women standing side by side facing us. The caption read: "The women fighters of the Ghetto Uprising, after capture, await their fate with resolution and dignity. In a moment shots will be fired." Mark Hurvitz, a member of *Davka*'s editorial review board and a future rabbi, had posters of the cover produced and stapled them to telephone poles all around the city.

Though *Davka*'s circulation hovered around 3,000 subscribers, the magazine quickly gained national and international attention for addressing neglected topics, such as the failure of Jewish religious schools to include the Holocaust in their curricula. An edition devoted to "The Forgotten Jews," dignified marginalized people in the community, including gays, prisoners, the poor, and the old.

When the *Encyclopedia Judaica* (1972–73 Yearbook) praised *Davka* for "fostering a Jewish cultural renaissance," I had already moved to Israel with the hope that I could somehow make my voice heard there as well.

— *marty* —

Revealing My *Aliyah* Plan

I'm not sure exactly when I declared to my parents my intention to make *aliyah*, immigrate to Israel. I must have alluded to it in my letters, though our correspondence rarely went beyond "How are you doing?" Just as they didn't disclose what was happening at home with my father's cancer, I revealed little of my Israel experience in the weekly aero-grammes I sent to them. Each of their letters contained a few red hearts drawn by my mom and on occasion by my father.

Once I was back in LA, we discussed my decision to make Israel my home. My mother expressed some reservations but made no attempt to dissuade me. My father greeted my decision with pride, even enthusiasm.

From as early as I can remember, Israel was regarded by the survivor community as the fulfillment of two thousand years of longing to return to our people's homeland. In our home, there were frequent references to my father's nephew Zvi and my mother's niece Bronka, who had immigrated to Israel after the war.

I asked my parents about their plans for the future. They were considering retirement, selling their business, and making *aliyah* to be near me. No surprise. What would keep them in LA when their only child would be living halfway around the world?

— *aron* —

Chutzpah

Merilyn was a semester behind me at UCLA. We decided that I would go to Israel ahead of her to set things up. I rented a three-bedroom flat on Rav Berlin Street in Jerusalem from my friend, Shlomo Dinur, an Israeli official tasked with reaching out to young Jews around the world. Shlomo believed that in my role as a writer and member of a group called the Radical Zionist Alliance (RZA), I was well positioned to encourage like-minded people to make *aliyah* to Israel.

One of RZA's key objectives, which I described in an interview on an English Israeli national radio program, was to transform Israeli society through the creation of *"irbutzim,"* urban kibbutzim. Here I was, a new immigrant who couldn't even hold a simple conversation in Hebrew, telling Israelis how to build a better society. Now that's chutzpah!

My Rav Berlin flat served as RZA world headquarters. It didn't take me long to realize that I was at the front of the line to nowhere. Rarely did anyone come knocking on my door. When someone did show up, I would sit them down with a cup of coffee and explain that the *irbutz* idea was but a dream. "If you are serious about living communally," I advised, "join a kibbutz."

The person I least expected to show up at my door was my sister.

In early June, just days after her eighteenth birthday, Rose hatched a secret plan calculated to win our parents' approval: to spend the summer on a kibbutz program. Rose didn't tell them or her boyfriend, Bitzy, that she had bought a one-way plane ticket to Israel with money Ma and Pop had given her as a high school graduation gift. Inspired by the autobiography of free-spirited dance legend Isadora Duncan, Rose set her sights on becoming a dancer, traveler, and seeker of knowledge. Her plan was to spend the summer on a kibbutz and then go to London or Paris.

Due to some snafu, Rose was unable to connect with the kibbutz program and instead moved in with me. One day while walking toward our flat on Rav Berlin, she happened upon the Rubin Academy of Music and Dance. She observed in the school's outdoor courtyard a few young dancers in leotards and tights stretching in the shade of a magnificent old olive tree. Curious to know more about the school, she entered the building, a former villa with elegant archways. The receptionist informed her that auditions for the upcoming school year were being held the following week.

Rose aced the auditions and was accepted on a full scholarship to study ballet and modern dance at Israel's premier conservatory for the performing arts. When she told our parents that she wouldn't be returning to LA anytime soon, Ma ordered her to come home immediately. Rose refused. When she wrote to Bitzy about her decision, he replied, "There's no point in pretending that we're together when you're there and I'm here." What Rose did was very gutsy. I loved having her close. Little did I know how much her presence would prove to be a source of great comfort to me in the difficult months ahead.

— *marty* —

Moving to Israel

Upon completing my BA in June 1970, I skipped UCLA's commencement ceremony. I had already figuratively checked out, focusing all my attention on moving to Israel. I did delay my departure by about a week to see the newly released film version of my favorite book, Joseph Heller's *Catch-22*. The underlying themes of the horror and absurdity of war weren't lost on me, but I was sure that what awaited me as an Israeli soldier would be nothing like what the book depicted.

In early July, my cousin Zvi picked me up from the airport and drove me to his apartment in Kfar Saba, where I would live until settled. I arranged for a three-month *ulpan* program at Kibbutz Maabarot, about an hour's drive away. This deeper immersion into Hebrew and reintroduction to kibbutz life were invaluable. I realized that, as welcoming and supportive as most of the members were, I had no appetite for communal living. It was an acquired taste that I had no interest in cultivating.

In accordance with Israel's Law of Return, Jewish immigrants are entitled to receive automatic citizenship after living in the country for at least three months. There was no conflict with US law. Not only did I become an Israeli citizen that summer, but I adopted my Hebrew name, Zvi, and in accordance with Israeli law, registered for military service. Shortly after I was notified of my scheduled induction into the Israel Defense Forces (IDF), a letter arrived from my draft board in the US informing me that my II-S student deferment had expired and that I had been reclassified I-A, draft eligible. I replied that I was an Israeli citizen, obligated and ordered to serve in the IDF, fulfilling my legal military duty. Never heard from the draft board again.

I spent countless hours with my Israeli family in their small apartment. Miriam continued to educate me in Israeli history. As much as the kids wanted to learn English from me, I always politely declined, preferring to practice my Hebrew with them.

— *aron* —

A Jab in the Heart

The postman delivered a letter from Merilyn with devastating news, a jab in the heart. She would not be coming to Israel after all. No reason given. Though I had thought we would be together for the rest of our lives, for some inexplicable reason I accepted her verdict as final. I didn't call or write to ask why she was breaking up with me or to reconsider her decision. Rose recalls, "You sat in your room in a near catatonic state for three days, trying to come to grips with the biggest loss of your life. It was your way of sitting *shiva* to mourn the death of your relationship with Merilyn."

Merilyn later explained to me that she had doubts about converting to Judaism without a compelling reason to forsake her own Polish heritage. She decided to visit Poland wearing a Star of David pendant around her neck to gauge for herself the degree of antisemitism in the land of her ancestors. The Poles failed the test. Merilyn later completed her conversion with Rabbi Richard Levy, the Hillel director, and adopted the name Ariel. She remained single but raised a son, Gabriel, in the Jewish faith and lived the rest of her life as a committed Jew.

Ariel's life ended in Los Angeles on December 18, 2012, following a three-year battle with brain cancer. She was sixty-three. Rose, who had remained one of Ariel's closest friends, delivered these words for me at Ariel's funeral:

> There was a shyness about her, coupled with a stunning sense of moral indignation about injustice anywhere in the world. I found her intriguing, but never imagined that a girl whose boyfriend was a Black Panther would ever go for a nice Jewish boy like me.
>
> Although Merilyn was not Jewish when we met, she was drawn to the Radical Jewish Community on campus, and I followed along. As she drew closer to Jewish culture, I became more political. Ariel was a woman of valor who lived her life with integrity, moral purpose, and extraordinary inner strength.

Inscribed on Ariel's gravestone is a Jewish star.

— *marty* —

Bootcamp

On November 10, 1970, I reported to the IDF induction base. I was equally excited and nervous. As uniforms, boots, and gear were distributed, I began chatting with the other recruits. It quickly became apparent that I was not a native Hebrew speaker, though most of them didn't make a big deal about it. Immigrants were always welcomed.

When one new friend asked me if I'd like a *mitzupeh* (a chocolate-coated wafer bar) from the canteen, I politely accepted and then asked him what it was. Learning new words, nuances, idioms, colloquialisms, and specific military terms became an ongoing objective throughout my army tenure. I practiced re-creating conversations in my mind, spotting my errors, and self-correcting as much as possible.

I spent about two weeks at the main army induction center while waiting to be assigned to a unit and a "career path." My records noted that I had a college degree in psychology, which made me an exception because most Israelis do their military service prior to university studies. Consequently, I was interviewed by the commander of the psychology branch, Lieutenant Colonel Benny Shallit, who spoke perfect English.

He invited me to join the group of field psychology units he had founded and said that I would be fast-tracked to officer candidate school. This sounded very appealing to me, and after taking a few days to think it over, I reported back to him that I was in and very excited.

Psychologists served as consultants to commanders in different branches of the army with the goal of optimizing each unit's functioning. I later understood this to include selecting the best personnel for different levels of command, assessing morale, providing feedback to commanders when they were functioning under extreme stress, and even offering ideas on how to improve the marksmanship of soldiers.

I started basic training at the beginning of December at the age of twenty-one. Most of the others were eighteen, with the exception of Pini, a thirty-eight-year-old kibbutznik who for some unknown reason hadn't yet done his military service. If I thought I had a bit of maturity over the other guys, Pini humbled me. On one run near the completion of the training I was too exhausted to go on. Pini encouraged me: "You can do it! You can do it!" He ran beside me until the end of the run. And I did it.

Not everyone was as enthusiastic as I was to serve. If someone didn't follow orders quickly enough, the punishment was for everyone to run laps around the base. If the same person kept making the same mistake, there were methods to encourage him to do better. One was called "a blanket." We were housed in large tents and slept on cots. When the repeat offender entered the tent after dark, we threw a blanket over him and proceeded to hit the blanket. This proved to be a reliable method of getting guys back in line.

Our basic training coincided with winter, which meant a hefty amount of rain. I was cold and wet most of the time. On our first bivouac training, which meant spending the night away from base, I quickly learned not to sleep with my head near the opening of the tent so as to avoid the "wake up kick" to the head from our superiors.

Grenade throwing exercises went like this: Our lieutenant would be about twenty meters ahead of our squad. Each of us would run to him, and he'd hand us a casing containing a live grenade. We'd remove it, yell "Grenade!" throw only the casing at a pair of barrels about twenty-five meters away, and then duck for cover. The first throw was a dry run. On my first throw, I completely missed the barrels. As I sulked back, the lieutenant turned to me and said sarcastically, "America." Well, on my next try, this time with the pin pulled, I threw the live grenade, yelled "Grenade!" and ducked. After the explosion, we both looked up and saw that one barrel had moved several feet. The grenade must have landed inside it and the force of the explosion had lifted and moved it. I turned to the lieutenant and in a similar tone said, "America." Quite satisfying.

After basic training, I had a hiatus of a few months before reporting to officer school. One of my tasks was documenting training procedures involving helicopters lifting and dropping off supplies to field units. During one night exercise, I found myself lifting off the ground in a chopper and directing a pilot where to land to perform these tasks—a little adventure for me, though I really didn't know what I was doing.

My parents had meanwhile liquidated their clothing store, made *aliyah*, and purchased an apartment in Kfar Saba near Zvi's family. We were united once again.

— *aron* —

My True Calling

When my friend Gerald Serotta decided to become a rabbi, he asked if I wanted to take over his job as editor of the Israeli branch of the Jewish Student Press Service (JSPS), a news organization that supplied articles to more than fifty campus publications in North America. Realizing that Jewish journalism was my true calling, I said yes.

As a registered foreign correspondent, I could travel the country in pursuit of stories to syndicate through JSPS. I was naturally drawn to some of the most controversial characters in the news. One afternoon, I took a bus to the Mea Shearim quarter of Jerusalem in search of Rabbi Amram Blau, the ultra-Orthodox founder of the militant anti-Zionist group Neturei Karta. An engraved sign outside his door read: "A Jew, not a Zionist" in English, Hebrew, and Arabic.

With his rotund frame and white silky hair, Reb Amram, as he was known, looked like a Hasidic Santa Claus. He was unexpectedly mild mannered. He made no fuss about my coming to his house without my head covered and responded calmly to my questions about his radical positions and activities. When I asked why his group so abhorred the State of Israel, he explained that establishing a Jewish state ahead of the coming of the Messiah was heresy and that the Holocaust was God's punishment. Though I found his answers shocking and I disagreed with everything he said in the interview, Reb Amram and I felt friendly toward one another. We would soon meet again under very different circumstances.

— *marty* —
IDF Officer

In June 1971, I reported to the officers course at a base in the Negev Desert. This was the beginning of four months of intensive training. Not only was it physically demanding, but gaps in my Hebrew made everything more difficult. I shared a room with five others. All but one were friendly and supportive. The lone holdout's animosity had nothing to do with me personally; he was just a mean-spirited guy. It brought home to me that Israelis were no different from people of any other nation. I encountered the good, the bad, and the ugly.

Upon graduating, I reported back to Lt. Col. Benny. He assigned me to a paratrooper unit, where I aided in identifying criteria for success among new recruits while accompanying them through basic training. Unfortunately, just before I was to go away to "jump school," my medical records revealed that I had elevated blood pressure, which precluded me from continuing in the paratrooper unit. The reading had been taken on the day of my induction. I was nervous at the time, probably driving up the numbers.

I was assigned to the Golani Brigade, an infantry unit. I'd be working alongside another psychologist named Moti, who was already a respected presence there. The home base was near Nahariya, a small city on Israel's northern Mediterranean coast.

My military obligations kept me from seeing much of my parents, which proved especially difficult when my father's cancer relapsed, this time in his lungs. He began to receive chemo treatments from an American doctor who was also an immigrant. My father struggled during his illness but never complained. I was usually able to be with my parents on Friday evenings and Saturdays, returning to my base on Sunday morning. As my father grew weaker and weaker, we spoke less and less about his condition.

During his last month of life, a nurse came twice daily to give him a morphine injection. Zvi and Miriam stepped in and were of enormous support. By then, I spent more days at home. On the night before my father died, Zvi and Miriam slept in our apartment. As my father lay dying, I could not bring myself to share any parting words with him. At about 5:00 a.m., I heard my mother scream, "He's cold! He's cold!" We all rushed to my father's side on the porch. He had passed. I was unable to comfort my mother and would not let her comfort me.

Members of the Jewish Religious Society, whose task it was to care for the deceased, lowered my father's body onto the floor. To keep it cold until his burial later in the day, they placed blocks of dry ice close to the head and feet. Zvi and Miriam arranged for notices of his death to appear in newspapers and around town, as was customary. I practiced reciting the Kaddish, the mourner's prayer. He was buried in accordance with Jewish tradition in the Kfar Saba cemetery. I was amazed to see so many people at the funeral, many of them strangers to me. Among the mourners was my father's former employer in New York who had laid him off, one of the reasons we moved to Los Angeles. I took his presence as an acknowledgement of my father's *shem tov*, good name.

— *aron* —

A Jerusalem Love Story

Still interested in communal living, I decided to make an exploratory visit to Kibbutz Adamit, a fledgling kibbutz in the north of the country populated by young people from various corners of the Diaspora. My sister accompanied me. While schmoozing with some of the kibbutz members, I mentioned that Rose and I were planning to travel around Europe that summer. One of them, Marcia Ente, said, "Oh, I have a friend who recently left the kibbutz who also will be going to Europe. Her name is Judy Hirt. She's living with her parents in Jerusalem. Would you like to meet her?" I said, "Sure" and didn't give it any more thought. A few days later, while checking my mail, I turned and caught a glimpse of Marcia Ente walking toward me with a beautiful woman dressed in a white embroidered Arab shirt that reached just above her knees.

Rose witnessed that moment of meeting: "You could see the electricity flying between Aron and Judy. It was love at first sight."

Judy had long brown hair with little braids framing her face. My ample black curls and long beard appealed to her. She thought my recycled herringbone jacket with suede elbow patches was cool. My ability to speak Yiddish turned out to be an asset. Judy had never met a natural Yiddish speaker her own age. She had learned the language as a child at the secular, progressive Peretz School in Vancouver, Canada.

Judy told me that she had moved to Israel a year earlier, largely because of her strong interest in ethnomusicology. She wanted to learn more about the diverse music and dance traditions brought by immigrants to Israel from across the Diaspora. Like me, she was attracted to the idea of communal living, which had led to her volunteering at two established kibbutzim before joining Adamit.

I invited Judy for Shabbat dinner. When she arrived, I rather innocently handed her a package of fresh ground meat, a couple of potatoes, and an onion. Judy hadn't planned on cooking but graciously prepared a delicious meal. Little did I know that she came from a family of superb chefs and bakers. A big plus.

The following weekend, Judy and I hosted a party at my Jerusalem apartment. A dozen Adamit members showed up and stayed the night, occupying all the beds and every inch of floor space. Judy and I decided to retreat to her parents' apartment. The following morning at the breakfast table, I was introduced to Judy's parents.

Concerned that I had not made a very good first impression and feeling intimidated by Judy's six-foot-two psychiatrist father, I gathered my courage and asked Dr. Hirt if we might have a word. He nodded and escorted me onto the balcony. "You know that Judy and I just met," I said, "but I promise you that I would never do anything to hurt her." He said, "Okay" and handed me one of his best Cuban cigars.

Judy was now faced with a fateful choice: to stay in Israel with me or follow through on her plan to return to North America in the fall to attend graduate school. With that decision in the balance, we spread a picnic blanket under an ancient olive tree in Jerusalem's Valley of the Cross. Surrounded by red poppies and other colorful wildflowers, we agreed that if Judy were to go back, there would be little chance of our relationship surviving from afar. Judy chose to stay in Israel.

Before embarking on our European vacation together, we rented an apartment on a quiet road between the Givat Ram campus of Hebrew University and the Israel Museum. By this time, I had come to admire Judy's many qualities, among them her kindness, insistence on excellence, intelligence, creativity, and ability (unlike me) to fix things.

After living together for a few months, we wrote letters to one another's parents (Judy's parents were back in Vancouver after Dr. Hirt's yearlong sabbatical in Israel) announcing that we had decided to get married and asking for their blessings. I was twenty-four and Judy, a year younger.

Eager to meet Judy and to finally set foot in the Jewish homeland, Ma came for a visit. The day after she arrived, she joined Judy and a couple of her friends on their weekly trip to the ancient Turkish hammam, a cavernous communal bath house located in Jerusalem's Bukharan Quarter. Ma brought along her bathing suit. She did not expect to see her future daughter-in-law naked. The steamy *shvitz* took a toll on Ma's bouffant, but her spirits remained high. Ma was thrilled with Judy, confident that the match was "meant to be."

Before returning home, Ma visited some of her survivor friends who had settled in Palestine after the liberation, including a reunion in Haifa with Tzipora Magerkewicz. The two women had shared a bunk in Grünberg and together escaped the death march.

During Ma's visit, Reb Amram and his French-born wife, Ruth, invited us for dinner. Ruth was widely known in Israel as "*hagiyoret*," the convert. She made headlines in the 1960s when it was revealed that she had abducted a young boy, Yossele Schumacher. The scheme was initiated by the boy's ultra-Orthodox grandparents who were opposed to his being raised by his non-religious parents. When I learned of Ruth's role in the conspiracy, I asked her to tell me her side of the story. My write-up appeared in a leading Israeli weekly magazine on May 5, 1973. Translated into Hebrew, the article revealed how Ruth had secreted Yossele out of the country disguised as a girl and how the Israeli Shin Bet finally trapped Ruth into confessing.

At the Blau dinner, my mother pulled out some photos from her purse. The first was one of me dressed for Purim as my hero, Theodor Herzl, the father of the modern Zionist movement. Apparently, Ma didn't realize that our anti-Zionist hosts might find the photo offensive. I blushed. Reb Amram and Ruth smiled. No harm done.

The sixteen months Judy and I lived together in Jerusalem was a time of relative calm. We felt safe walking through the Old City on Saturdays, making friends with Arab merchants in the *shuk*, market, who served us glasses of mint tea and Turkish coffee. And we never missed an opportunity to stop at our favorite bakery for a couple squares of knafeh, a delicious, orange-colored cheese pastry soaked in sweet syrup and topped with shredded dough.

Before leaving Israel in the summer of 1973, we held a "yard sale" in front of the Old City's Jaffa Gate. Sales of our blue jeans, books, records, and kitchenware were going well until a cop shut us down for operating without a license. On the way to the airport, we stopped in Kfar Saba to say goodbye to Marty, never imagining that, come Yom Kippur, his army unit would be fighting Syrian forces on the Golan Heights.

— *marty* —

Yom Kippur War

On Yom Kippur, October 6, 1973, I was in my Ramat Gan apartment listening to rock 'n' roll music broadcast from Abie Nathan's "Peace Ship," anchored just outside Israeli territorial waters.

Suddenly, at 2:00 p.m., sirens began to sound. I glanced out the window and saw several men clad in prayer shawls outside a synagogue. They looked confused. I turned on the radio and heard that Egypt and Syria had launched a surprise attack on Israel. We were at war!

I quickly put on my uniform, packed a few things, including my Uzi, and headed to the nearest military base, where it was apparent that Israel had been caught totally off guard. Amidst the confusion, two other officers jumped into my jeep, and we set out to the home base of our infantry brigade near Nahariya in the north. Upon arrival, we learned a few more details about what was happening. Advancing Syrian forces had penetrated our lines on the Golan Heights.

Facing my first experience of war, I had no idea what to expect. Any fear I might have felt was tempered by an edge of enthusiasm, of being in action, of moving forward.

By nightfall, we found ourselves in a long convoy of slow-moving military vehicles, headlights off, making our way onto the Golan Heights. Upon arrival at our base at Nafach we tried to get an update on the situation, but no one could give us an accurate assessment because everything was changing so fast on the ground. One of the buildings served as an aid station. This was my first encounter with casualties. I was shocked to see so many bloodied bodies.

The rapid advance of Syrian and Egyptian forces shattered the sense of invincibility that many Israelis had felt since their stunning victory in the 1967 Six-Day War. As a field psychologist, my duty was to assist commanders in optimizing combat functioning. This meant preparing soldiers to do most efficiently what they were ultimately trained to do: kill the enemy. Only after the war did I begin to grasp how diametrically opposed this task was to my fundamental relationship with psychology, which was predicated on helping, supporting, and empowering people in their lives. Now, in the midst of a war of survival, I and everyone around me focused only on defeating the enemy.

The line of half-tracks transporting us toward our forward fortifications came under constant artillery fire. A hailstorm of sharp, jagged pieces of shrapnel struck our vehicle. I was under the misconception that the armor on our half-track could actually shield us. Any illusion of invincibility I may have had going into battle ended when I witnessed the carnage of a direct hit. It was unnerving not knowing whether the whistling noise of the next incoming mortar shell would be the last sound I would ever hear.

The following evening, our Golani Brigade commander convened the officers and explained that our objective was to retake the northernmost position atop Mt. Hermon. The Syrians who had captured this fortification on the first day of the war had repelled our first attempt. Integral to my job as one of the brigade's two field psychologists was to cultivate strong, trusting relationships at all levels with commanders. The battalion commander with whom I had the most congenial relationship, even friendship, was Lt. Colonel Dubi Dror. I was at the casualty aid position when I learned that Dubi had been killed during a second attempt to retake the fortification. Someone shouted out that assistance was needed to remove his body from a half-track. I did not respond, a failure I would deeply regret for many years.

After five days, our troops initiated a coordinated counterattack of armor, artillery, and infantry that pierced Syria's border defenses. Moti, the other brigade psychologist, and I drove behind the advancing forces. From a distance we saw what appeared to be men dressed in red. As we got closer, they turned out to be our guys in uniforms covered in blood. They were removing the bodies of our soldiers from the battlefield in accordance with Jewish law requiring that all human remains be gathered and buried with the body as quickly as possible.

For a few days during the second week of the war, several of us psychologists were assigned to interact with a tank brigade and an artillery battery that were hit particularly hard during their time on the front lines. The artillery battery had been overrun by Syrian forces and suffered a casualty rate of about 90 percent. The soldiers from these units were brought to a kibbutz in the north. Our job was to give them an opportunity to talk about what they were feeling, but almost no one was willing to interact with us. They just sat in silence, staring at the walls or ceiling. All we could do was to be present and available to listen. This closing down of emotions brought to mind my family's reluctance to talk about the Holocaust.

After two weeks our forces succeeded in pushing back the Syrian army to within thirty kilometers of Damascus. At a debriefing conducted by the new acting brigade commander (the former had been wounded), we learned how many troops in our units had been killed, wounded, and how many weapons and rounds of ammunition remained in our arsenal. These statistics were presented absent emotion, just read aloud. The casualty figures included several men I knew well. I could feel myself hardening, closing up, burying my emotions. My idealized conception of the glorious Israel Defense Forces was quickly losing its hold on me.

As I was driving home from the battlefront, a young man tried to pass me recklessly. I forced him off the road and flew into a rage, nearly pulling him from his car for a thrashing. I was out of control. I didn't recognize myself.

About a week later, sitting alone in my apartment, I made a voice recording of my war experiences. I listened to it a couple of times and shared it with no one. My voice sounded sad and gloomy. Over the years, the tape disappeared. I don't miss it.

I spent some of December and January across the Suez Canal in the areas of Egypt we had taken. It was there that I shaved off my beard in accordance with a Southern Command-wide order to ensure that a mask would fit over my face hermetically in the event of gas warfare. Such an attack never occurred.

During the last year and a half of my military service, I left the field unit and worked at a base near Tel Aviv doing psychological assessment of soldiers for officer candidate school. Coming home every evening after work, I began to feel a sense of normalcy.

— *aron* —

Vancouver Wedding

Wanting our marriage experience to be traditional, Judy immersed herself in a *mikveh*, ritual bath, and recited the blessings for a bride. We then met with the local Reform rabbi, who surprised us by expressing opposition to the groom stomping on a glass at the end of the ceremony. What bothered him was the act's supposed sexual symbolism—the breaking of the hymen. Judy and I had a different take on the custom, one aligned with the traditional interpretation: Even at the most joyous of occasions, Jews are obliged to remember the destruction of the Temples in Jerusalem and other historical catastrophes that have befallen our people. We decided to ask our friend Orthodox Rabbi Moshe Adler to fly up from LA and co-officiate. He was the husband of Rachel Adler, who two years earlier had written the lead article in *Davka* magazine's issue on Jewish women.

On August 19, 1973, Judy and I were wed in the beautiful sunken garden of the Hirt home in Vancouver amid giant rhododendrons, dahlias, and roses of every color, bordered by flowering rock plants. The honor of holding the four corners of the *chuppah* was given to two of Judy's cousins; to our best man, Noah benShea; and to Rose's future husband, Bitzy Eichenbaum. Judy selected the ceremonial music. Two of her friends played the Hebrew song "Erev Shel Shoshanim" (Evening of Roses) on Japanese instruments, the koto and shakuhachi, as our parents accompanied us to the *chuppah*. We exchanged vows, I shattered the glass, and we were lifted onto chairs as family and friends danced the hora around us to a lively recording by the Jewish Greek band Kol Salonika.

Our only regret was that Judy had immersed herself in an unsanitary *mikveh*, resulting in her contending with tonsillitis on our wedding day.

Dr. Hirt's prescription of Scotch mixed with Drambuie did little to ease Judy's symptoms, though none of the guests would have guessed that she was sick.

Judy slowly recovered during our honeymoon, courtesy of Norman and Hannah Hirt, at Harrison Hot Springs, a resort about eighty miles from Vancouver. Men were required to wear a tie to dinner. I didn't have one. The maitre d' refused to seat us. Ever resourceful, Judy asked me to hand her one of my shoelaces. She converted it into a string tie. Problem solved.

After the wedding we moved into a one-bedroom apartment in my parents' building on North Spaulding Avenue. Judy's mother advised Ma and Pop that it was a good idea to charge us some rent (we shouldn't be *schnorrers*, freeloaders). They bought into the idea and charged us a token fifty dollars per month. Some of my parent's survivor friends had organized a bridal shower for Judy at the Beverly Hilton Hotel, providing us with a treasure trove of household goods, including a set of orange porcelain cookware (a gift from Judy's three great aunts and uncles who lived in our West Hollywood neighborhood), and a Hoover vacuum cleaner.

Judy had the good fortune of studying with one of the pioneers of dance therapy, Trudi Schoop. The Swiss-born comic mime, dancer, and author lived in a wooded artists' colony in the Valley about a thirty-minute drive from our home. With Trudi agreeing to be her mentor, Judy enrolled and completed a "university without walls" master's program through Goddard College. For her field work, Judy taught children with autism in a program run by the Exceptional Children's Foundation in Los Angeles. She had heard about the position from my ex-girlfriend, Ariel Malek. They worked together as teachers for two years.

To help cover our rent and other living expenses Judy and I taught at an innovative Jewish teen program called Havurat Noar. The curriculum was divided between weekly classes in designated synagogues and monthly weekend retreats at a Jewish camp.

I resumed my position as editor of *Davka*. To become a credible and knowledgeable Jewish writer and editor, I decided to pursue a formal Jewish studies program or possibly rabbinical ordination. When I mentioned the idea of becoming a rabbi to Pop, he frowned. Looking at my long beard, he may have pictured me in the image of the Hasidic rebbes he had known in Poland whose most fervent appeals to the Almighty proved powerless to stop the Nazis. I had my own reasons. I was not into God or prayer and didn't want to be cast in the role of anyone's spiritual surrogate. Besides, I had found my calling in Jewish journalism.

Where to study? I underlined two possibilities in the local phonebook: the University of Judaism (Conservative Judaism) and the Hebrew Union College-Jewish Institute of Religion (Reform Judaism). I dialed HUC-JIR first because I had a connection with Rabbi Bill Cutter, director of the Rhea Hirsch School of Education. He had written an article for *Davka*. When I told him of my reason for applying, he ushered me into the program on full scholarship and agreed that editing the magazine would satisfy my fieldwork requirement. I wrote my master's thesis on the publications of the Union of American Hebrew Congregations (UAHC), traveling to New York to meet and interview the organization's director of publications and editors.

On January 30, 1976, Judy gave birth to our first child, Noah. A few months later, I received my master's in Jewish Education. What next? One option was to remain in Los Angeles and become Dr. Cutter's eventual successor at HUC-JIR. A second possibility was to move to New York and become heir apparent to Jesse Lurie, executive editor of the preeminent Jewish magazine at the time: *Hadassah*. I went with a third option: editor of *Reform Judaism*, the official publication of the UAHC—for three reasons. As a HUC-JIR graduate, I was already a Reform Movement insider. The organization's newsprint periodical was in dire need of a makeover both graphically and editorially. Little chance of failing. And the position would afford me a huge platform to investigate topics of special interest to me, such as the long-neglected area of educating people about the Holocaust.

Totally focused on my career, I had given little thought to how Ma and Pop might take the news of our family relocating to New York. I did not discourage them from thinking that the move would be short lived. They had no concept of Jewish journalism as a profession. And besides, who in their right mind would want to trade paradise for the frigid east coast? They figured we'd be back in a year or two. It took me five years to make peace with the idea of not returning to Los Angeles. Had I known in 1976 how much Pop's health would decline after we left for New York, I would probably have applied for the administrative position at HUC-JIR in Los Angeles.

— *marty* —

Swap Meet Man

After serving in the Israel Defense Forces for five years, I was ready for a change. The vision that had drawn me to Israel so powerfully had become clouded by my war experience. Israel the dream and Israel the reality were now out of sync for me. I also knew that my mother felt very alone living in Kfar Saba and that reuniting her with Aunt Aga and Uncle Lolek would be good for them all. In August of 1975, one week after my release from the army, my mother and I returned to Los Angeles.

I enrolled in an MA program in psychology at California State University, which I completed in just a year while working the graveyard shift at a psychiatric halfway house in Santa Monica. I rented a room in Venice Beach, spending hours on end gazing out the window at the Pacific Ocean. My biggest daily decision was whether to eat in or order the breakfast special at Nupars, a nearby eatery.

While I was in Israel, Cousin Irving dropped out of Caltech and became somewhat of a bum. For a short while he even sold drugs. My father did what he could to help Irving, showing him more patience and kindness than did anyone else in the family. I had pretty much written him off.

By the time I came home, Irving had managed to clean up his act by going back to school. We even found ourselves in the same MA program in psychology at California State University. When I told Irving that my money was running out, he invited me to join him in the swap meet business. Another cousin, Sammy, who owned a clothing store on Hollywood Boulevard, provided the merchandise.

The first time out, Irving and I filled the trunk of his car with 360 men's shirts, which cost us two dollars apiece. We spent Friday night in the car, waiting in line to get a choice spot at a swap meet site at the Orange Drive-In Theater. We worked Saturday and Sunday and came home with fistfuls of cash. We turned this into a profitable business, opening and operating several locations around Los Angeles, Orange County, and San Diego. I treated myself to a Cadillac Seville, a nice apartment on Melrose Avenue, a color TV, and a top-of-the-line stereo system.

After a couple of years, Irving and I divided up the seven different swap meets we operated together and I moved to San Diego. Had my father still been alive, he would not have been thrilled about his bright son becoming the proverbial Jewish peddler. I had become a *luftmensch*, an aimless air person.

I had little communication with Aron during this period. I didn't even know that he had moved to New York.

chapter four

Finding Our Way

Career, Marriage, and Loss

— *aron* —

1976

In advance of moving my family to New York, I spent a week scouting the city for an apartment. Manhattan was out of our price range. Finding the seemingly endless rental listings in the Sunday *New York Times* intimidating, I asked myself what my immigrant parents would have done. Reach out to the survivor network.

Ma connected me with Regina Rottner, a childhood friend from Dabrowa who lived in Forest Hills, Queens. Over a glass of tea and mandel bread cookies, Regina sold me on Forest Hills as a family-friendly place. Having narrowed my search, I found a listing in a Jewish newspaper for the upper floor of a duplex. The landlords, Rita and Seymour Tiras, lived downstairs. They loved that I would be working for a Jewish organization and welcomed me like family. I signed a lease that very day and returned to Los Angeles to prepare for our cross-continent drive.

To ensure that we would be traveling in the safest car on the road, I bought a used Volvo from a professor at an affordable price. He warned me that under no circumstances would he take it back. I should have taken a hint, but my characteristic reliance on *mazel*, luck, clouded my judgment.

We drove up the coast to Vancouver to visit with Judy's family, spending a few extra days there while the Volvo was in the shop for a costly valve job. We then made our way across Canada to visit Judy's uncles and cousins. In Toronto the lemon needed a second valve job, nearly bankrupting us.

On my first day at the Union of American Hebrew Congregations I wore a white Indian cotton tunic with matching pants. Edie Miller, assistant to the president, Rabbi Alexander Schindler, said I looked like the ice cream man. The next day, I walked in wearing a thrift shop suit accessorized with a brownish green leatherette attaché case. Eleanor Schwartz, director of the National Federation of Sisterhoods, turned to me in the elevator and said, "Aron, take my advice and get yourself some decent clothes."

No one objected to my long black beard. When the Union's Board of Trustees next met, Rabbi Schindler announced, "I am pleased to report that Theodor Herzl has joined the staff as editor of *Reform Judaism*." Everyone got the joke. I really did look like a reincarnation of the Viennese journalist who founded the modern Zionist movement. I took a bow.

What mattered most to me was editorial freedom. Would I be allowed to continue the *Davka* tradition of breaking Jewish idols? To my relief, both Rabbi Schindler and Albert Vorspan, *Reform Judaism*'s executive editor and a champion of civil rights and social justice, took a respectful hands-off approach. I got the feeling that they actually wanted me to stir things up.

Best of all, they had no objection to my featuring Holocaust-related stories in the editorial mix. Rabbi Schindler, I later learned, was born in Munich, a short distance from Feldafing, my birthplace. He was twelve when his family fled Nazi Germany in 1937. He joined the US Army and was awarded both a Purple Heart and a Bronze Star for action in Italy during World War II.

Al Vorspan had joined the US Navy and survived a Japanese kamikaze attack on his ship in the Pacific. In the 1950s, Al provided office space to Raphael Lemkin, an impoverished lawyer of Polish-Jewish descent who coined the term "genocide" and devoted his life to the ratification of the Genocide Convention.

With the backing of my new bosses, I felt empowered to break new ground, particularly in exposing Nazi war criminals and those who engineered their escape from justice.

Rabbi Schindler's successor as president, Rabbi Eric Yoffie, continued the tradition of not interfering with my editorial decisions, though he did ask me to give less prominence to Holocaust-related content after a spring 2001 cover story by another son of survivors, Edwin Black, exposed how IBM technology aided the Nazis in the genocide of European Jewry. Rabbi Yoffie favored stories that focused more on the joys of contemporary religious practice than on history, more on the celebrative than on the lachrymose.

His successor, Rabbi Rick Jacobs, who became Union for Reform Judaism (URJ) president in 2012, expressed no such reservations, perhaps because of an experience he had several years earlier while senior rabbi at Westchester Reform Temple in Scarsdale, New York.

He had joined a mission organized by the American Jewish World Service (AJWS) to the African nation of Chad, where survivors of the genocide across the border in the Darfur region lived under horrifying conditions. Writing in a *Reform Judaism* magazine (Summer, 2006), Rabbi Jacobs drew parallels between the mass murder in Darfur and the Holocaust. "If we do nothing," he wrote, "then we forfeit our right to condemn the world's silence when our people faced hell on earth in Nazi-occupied Europe." Upon their return, the group initiated an AJWS campaign to raise consciousness and money in support of the refugees. Among Rabbi Jacobs' most cherished possessions is a *tallit* made of purple, gray, and silver fabric that he purchased in Chad "to remind me daily of our Darfurian brothers and sisters."

My tenure as an editor for the Union of American Hebrew Congregations (renamed Union for Reform Judaism 2003) would span forty-five years.

EST

I was living in San Diego and about to begin a PhD program in psychology when my girlfriend at the time introduced me to something called "est" (Erhard Seminars Training). She kept telling me how much of a difference the course had made in her life, but I would have nothing of it. I considered myself too smart, too experienced, too smug to have anything to do with a hyped seminar that promised in only two weekends to "transform one's ability to experience living so that the situations one had been trying to change or had been putting up with clear up just in the process of life itself." Then one afternoon a trusted swap meet buddy told me that he had done the est training and thought it would do me good. Trying not to "overthink" what this experience might be and figuring I had little to lose, I registered for the October 1979 est training program in Los Angeles.

The two weekend and three evening training sessions proved to be among the most profound experiences of my life. In only a matter of days, I was able to glimpse behind the curtain of my life and clearly see things that for years I had been trying to change or had resigned myself to endure. I began the training with an intention to clarify what I wanted to do with my life. The experience resulted in nothing less than a transformation.

I was able to stop invalidating myself for not helping to carry the body of my comrade Dubi during the Yom Kippur War. I was able to forgive myself for not being closer to my father during his illness, for not expressing my deep love for him, for not being able to ease his suffering. I was able to give him a posthumous hug and say, "I love you." I felt more grounded and ready to live my life without the shackles of fear and uncertainty.

The morning after completing the est training, I realized that much of what I wanted to accomplish as a psychologist was more expediently realized in just two weekends. I withdrew from the PhD program and became heavily involved with est, first as a volunteer and later as a staff member. With more training, I became effective at leading seminars and producing large events around the country and the world. In December of 1980 I had the privilege of producing the first est training in Israel.

— aron —

The Biggest Scoop

One morning in the winter of 1983, a large envelope appeared on my desk. The sender was Charles Allen Jr., an investigative journalist and former US military intelligence officer who specialized in tracking down escaped Nazi war criminals. The envelope contained a copy of a 1947 declassified top secret report by a US foreign service official named Vincent La Vista. It documented how Vatican operatives spirited high-ranking Nazi war criminals to South America. The escapees included Adolf Eichmann, who ran the logistics of the Holocaust (to Argentina); Franz Stangl, commandant of the Treblinka death camp (to Brazil); and Walter Hermann Julius Rauff, who invented the mobile gas vans used in the extermination of 1.4 million Jews in Nazi-occupied USSR (to Chile).

Realizing we had an enormous scoop, I assigned Allen the story and together we set about exposing the scandalous actions of one of the most powerful religious organizations in the world.

The La Vista Report described the activities of more than twenty relief and welfare organizations in Rome with ties to the Vatican that played a role in the rescue of fascist war criminals. It remained undetermined whether Pope Pius XII was aware of these clandestine activities.

Meanwhile, the US Counter Intelligence Corps (CIC) was running its own underground escape operation, "rat lines," designed to relocate Nazi war criminals whom they employed as spies after the war. A case in point was Klaus Barbie, known as the "Butcher of Lyon," who oversaw the deportation of thousands of French Jews to Nazi death camps. The CIC paid him to run a spy network in the US-occupied zone of Germany. When his services were no longer needed, he was given false papers and secreted through the "rat lines" to Genoa, Italy, where a priest operating within the Vatican secured a Bolivian visa for him.

Allen's story appeared in the summer/spring 1983 edition of *Reform Judaism* and made headlines across the globe, including the *New York Times*.

— *marty* —

Cracks in the Wall

In May of 1984, I traveled to Atlanta, Georgia, to supervise the first weekend of an est training program. At our Friday evening logistics meeting, I was immediately attracted to the woman heading up the volunteer team: Marti Ward. I assigned her numerous tasks of various complexity. In every case, she said, "I'll handle it," and she did. The event began on the morning of Saturday, May 19. At noon, during the first break, I pointed out Marti to the lead trainer and said, "I'm going to marry her."

Something changed in me that weekend in Atlanta. In the past, I had always steered clear of marriage. I vaguely suspected the reason was Holocaust related. I could not imagine myself being able to endure the loss of a wife and children. The most certain way to avoid such an unbearable scenario was never to start a family. Meeting Marti somehow helped me overcome this fear.

I hadn't planned on seeing her again anytime soon, but fate intervened. The following week, I got a desperate call from Fran, the Atlanta est center manager. She needed me back for the second weekend because the scheduled supervisor couldn't make it. At the time I was in San Antonio, Texas, helping a friend who was moving there from Los Angeles. I jumped at the opportunity, striking a deal with Fran. "I'll do it," I said, "if you reimburse me for the clothes I'll need to buy and all travel costs." When I phoned Marti to tell her that I was returning to Atlanta, she shared my enthusiasm about being together again. By the end of the weekend, we agreed that this turn of events was no accident.

In the weeks that followed, Marti and I spoke by phone daily. I learned that she had grown up a Baptist in western Maryland. She was the divorced mother of a five-year-old daughter named Andrea. She owned and operated an aerobic fitness studio and a hair salon in Charleston, South Carolina.

Her not being Jewish was a non-issue. What mattered to me was our shared values and our commitment to making a difference in the world. Three weeks later, I arrived in Charleston with an engagement ring. I just knew that she was the one.

— *aron* —

East Germany

The revelation in *Reform Judaism* of the Vatican's role in assisting escaped Nazi war criminals caught the attention of officials in communist East Germany. I was invited along with two other Jewish journalists to tour the German Democratic Republic (GDR). For ten days, we were escorted around the country by a personable Jewish guide named Werner Handler, likely an agent of Stasi, the internal security force.

Not much of a Jewish community remained in the GDR. Funerals far outnumbered births in this community of 600 mostly elderly members with no rabbi, cantor, or religious schools. Yet the government financed the Jewish community, refurbishing or rebuilding eight synagogues and maintaining Jewish cemeteries. It wouldn't look good for a regime that had supposedly eradicated antisemitism and fascism to become *Judenrein*, cleansed of Jews.

We visited the Rykestrasse Synagogue in East Berlin. A section of its library contained forbidden books available only to scholars: Nazi literature, including Adolf Hitler's *Mein Kampf*, and Zionist literature, including *The Diaries of Theodor Herzl*. When we stepped back into the main room of the library, a Jewish man whispered into my ear: "Don't believe a word they are telling you. It is a terrible life for us here. Please help me get to Israel."

We toured the former concentration camp sites of Buchenwald, Ravensbrück, and Sachsenhausen, which the government used for ideological indoctrination. School children were taught that Nazism was the logical extension of capitalism and that concentration camps utilized forced labor to enrich West German industrialists. There was no mention that Jews were singled out for annihilation.

The denial of Jewish victimization extended to the arts. After viewing a stage performance of *The Diary of Anne Frank* in Leipzig, I asked the young blonde woman who played Anne if at any point she had imagined her character as Jewish. She replied, "I just try to portray a girl in that situation." In her mind, Anne Frank being Jewish was irrelevant. Anne was simply a victim of fascist aggression.

On our last day in the GDR, we attended a performance of *Fiddler on the Roof* at the Komische Oper Berlin. It had been running for four years straight to sold-out audiences. There were no Jews in the cast. As the actors sang, "Tradition, Tradition" in German, I surveyed the audience of mostly white-haired people and felt the urge to scream out, "It was *you* who tried to destroy the very tradition you now find so delightful!" I then imagined myself being dragged off to a psychiatric ward by Stasi agents.

As we prepared to depart the GDR, one of Werner Handler's comrades handed me a sealed envelope and asked that I post it in Manhattan. It was a curious request. There was regular mail service between the two countries. I took the envelope, thinking that the Stasi was testing me.

Not for a minute did I buy into the East German view that they were the good guys in the struggle against fascism. The press tour convinced me that totalitarianism on the left is just as repugnant as it is on the right.

I discarded the envelope unopened. A week after our return home, Werner inquired if I had posted it in New York. I told him that it somehow got lost en route. So ended my surreal GDR adventure.

— *marty* —

Marti Meets My Family

Not long after arriving in Charleston Marti and I went out to dinner at the Lodge Valley Inn. I presented her with the ring and asked her to marry me. Without hesitation she said yes.

We then flew to Los Angeles so that Marti could meet my family. Just as I knew instantly that Marti would be an extraordinary soulmate, I had no doubt that she would be accepted lovingly by my family. My mother and Aunt Aga embraced Marti straightaway, recognizing what a jewel of a human being she is. I'm quite sure they were happy that at age thirty-four I had finally found a woman to marry.

Uncle Lolek, though a self-declared agnostic, let Marti know in a most hospitable manner that he would "recognize" her as a member of the family only after she converted to Judaism. Marti was absolutely fine with his terms, and he delivered on his promise.

My father's older brother, Jack, was hospitalized at the time. When we visited him, I was impressed by how gently Marti stroked his forehead as he lay in bed. Jack passed away a short time later.

Marti was warmly welcomed by my friends as well. My est seminar leader friends in LA treated me to a "grits party" to grease the slide for my move to the South. We returned to Charleston and were married at midnight on August 1, 1984, on Sullivan's Island Beach in the presence of friends and a justice of the peace. The following morning I was off to Atlanta, then to Houston for the weekend, where I attended an est seminar leaders' weekend training. Marti joined me in Houston, spending what we referred to as our honeymoon, sort of working.

Though I didn't consider myself religious, Marti understood that I could never be anything but Jewish. Having always had an affinity for Jewish people, Marti decided to convert to Judaism as a statement of unity and solidarity with me, my family, and my people. The appropriateness of this action was clear to us both. She began the conversion process with a rabbi in Charleston. One year later, on August 4, 1985, at my mother's request, we had a Jewish wedding ceremony in Los Angeles.

In our family, Marti is the one who initiates holiday traditions. She bakes the best challah I've ever tasted, prepares a first-rate matzah ball soup, and for our Passover seders, outstanding gefilte fish from scratch!

— *aron* —

The Promise

Our family had grown since we moved to New York. Noah was four when his brother, Isaac, was born on Long Island. We had bought a fixer-upper in Port Washington, having raised the down payment from parental contributions and settlement money from a car accident. Judy was driving our Toyota Corolla with Rose in the passenger seat on Laurel Canyon Boulevard in LA when a drunk driver in a large sedan crashed into them head on. Judy suffered a broken pelvis and cracked sacrum. She was hospitalized for two weeks. Rose's injuries were less serious. The Corolla was totaled.

Our third child, Miriam (Mimi), was born in Connecticut, where we bought a house on more than two acres of land with the aim of growing a huge vegetable garden. Our life on the East Coast had certainly taken root. It seemed that I would be working at the Union for the foreseeable future. California kept receding farther and farther into the rearview.

Ma and Pop did not make me feel guilty about our living so far away from them. Pop had only one request: that I shave off my beard because it made him feel old. He even offered me a cash reward. I refused. To ensure that my marriage to Judy would endure, he instructed Ma to give us $100 each year on our anniversary. She honored his wish and it worked. We just surpassed the $5,100 mark.

Shortly after Mimi's birth, I visited my family in Los Angeles. At the time, Pop was housed at the Brier Oak Terrace, a short-stay rehabilitation facility on Sunset Boulevard. I didn't realize how much Pop's health had deteriorated since he collapsed in the street about a year earlier and was rushed by ambulance to Cedars-Sinai Hospital. Unaware of his compromised pulmonary history, ER doctors pumped him with too much oxygen. After that, Pop could not breathe without being connected to some form of respiratory apparatus.

I wasn't prepared for what I witnessed at the facility. In Pop's case, it was a halfway house between life and death. After navigating a labyrinth of narrow hallways, I found Pop's cubicle. A tall oxygen tank flanked his bed. He smiled as I entered, but his blue eyes betrayed a deep sadness. To cheer him up, I showed him a photo of his new granddaughter. He nodded approvingly, unable to speak because of a tracheostomy tube in his throat. Before leaving, I asked Pop if there was anything he wanted me to do for him. He motioned me to come close and whispered, *"Farges nisht meine yahrzeit"* (Don't forget the anniversary of my death). I promised with a kiss.

A few weeks later, on October 10, 1984, on the eve of the Jewish holiday of Sukkot, Pop died of respiratory failure. He was sixty-nine.

— *marty* —
Southern Living

Marti lived in a rented house in Mount Pleasant, a suburb of Charleston. This was my new home. Driving down the main street, I noticed a supermarket with a strange and amusing name: "Piggly Wiggly." Nothing like that in California.

We often spent time in Charleston, attracted by the charm of this historic city. To preserve its character, the municipality strictly regulated the colors of its modest buildings. We visited nearby sprawling plantations, which had been repurposed from bastions of slavery into venues for concerts and tours. Charleston is also home to one of the nation's first synagogues: Kahal Kadosh Beth Elohim, established in 1749.

I had never considered even visiting the South, which I associated with the 1964 murder in Mississippi of three civil rights volunteers: James Chaney, Michael Schwerner, and Andrew Goodman. This incident, more than any other short of the Holocaust, stood out in my mind as the brutality human beings were capable of inflicting on those deemed to be "other." I wanted no part of an environment where as a Jew I might find myself in jeopardy.

Living in the South, my stereotypical thinking began to change. In the past, my sense of safety in the company of others was predicated primarily on whether they were Jewish. It was a tribal connection rooted in an ancient bond. Through est I learned to connect with people as people, regardless of affiliation. What mattered was a shared commitment to loving kindness, to making a difference in life, and an openness to possibilities. These attributes became the foundation of how I now related to others, including Marti and my five-year-old stepdaughter, Andrea. I had no template for the role of father. It took me a while to feel more at ease as Marti's parenting partner. Over time, Andrea began to call me "Daddy." She had a relationship with her biological father but recognized that I was there for her mom and for her. When her biological dad died in a bike accident a few years later, I became the sole father figure in her life.

— *aron* —

Becoming an Author

After Pop died, I no longer considered moving back to Los Angeles and recommitted myself to my job. As a side gig, I served as editor-in-chief of The Holocaust Library, a publishing house founded in the 1950s by Holocaust survivors during a period when American publishers shunned the subject. As editor, I worked with Elie Wiesel on his three-volume collection *Against Silence: The Voice and Vision of Elie Wiesel* (Holocaust Library, 1985).

I was yet to see my name on the cover of a book. My chance came one afternoon in the winter of 1988, when I received a call from HarperCollins editor Carol Cohen. She told me that Bonny Fetterman, senior editor of Schocken Books, had recommended me as a Holocaust expert.

As proof of my bona fides, I presented Carol with a letter of recommendation from Elie Wiesel dated July 15, 1986, just three months before he was awarded the Nobel Peace Prize. In it he described me as "a man well-versed in Jewish history" and as "a writer possessed of a rare blend of integrity, persuasiveness, and good literary sense." I got the job.

Cohen asked me to authenticate a manuscript written by Siegfried Jagendorf, a survivor who claimed to have saved the lives of thousands of Romanian Jews exiled to Ukraine in 1941. Following the death of his widow, a copy of Jagendorf's memoir on onion skin paper had been discovered in a closet among other memorabilia. I agreed to look into the matter, though I had never heard of Jagendorf.

I consulted Elie Wiesel. Unfamiliar with Jagendorf, he referred me to Ion Butnaro, a historian of the Romanian Holocaust. Butnaro confirmed that Jagendorf had been a Jewish ghetto official in Moghilev-Podolski, a town in a Nazi-occupied territory of Ukraine known as Transnistria. Yet it remained a mystery as to whether "Engineer Jangendorf" was a savior or a collaborator intent on covering up his wartime activities.

I reported my initial findings to Cohen and advised her that Jagendorf's credibility would need to be substantiated. With the blessings of Jagendorf's heirs, I was hired as a kind of forensic editor tasked with determining how Jagendorf's name would go down in history. For the next two years, I spent many a weekend in Boston with Butnaro going over copies of documents in Romanian and German that he had brought back for me from the Jagendorf Archives at Yad Vashem in Jerusalem.

In Akron, Ohio, I interviewed Jagendorf's two daughters, Elfreda Stern and Edith Gitman, who described their family's prewar years in Romania. Having escaped to the United States before their parents were swept up in the mass deportation of Romanian Jews to Transnistria, they had no first-hand knowledge of how their father conducted himself as the director of the Turnatoria, the foundry he and his hand-picked crew of Jewish deportees restored after it had been sabotaged by retreating Soviet forces.

I got my first break when Edith and Elfreda told me that two people whose lives their father had saved would be traveling from Paris to Port Washington, Long Island, to attend a wedding. Rifka and Arnold Auerbach agreed to meet with me, but when I took out my tape recorder, they ordered me to put it away. Perplexed, I asked them if it was true, as Siegfried Jagendorf wrote in his memoir, that he had rescued Arnold from a firing squad after Rifka, a Turnatoria worker, had implored him to intervene with the gendarme commander. They confirmed the accuracy of Jagendorf's account but would have nothing to do with the book because, in their words, "He behaved like a dictator and Romanian guards saluted him."

After months of research and still uncertain about Jagendorf's wartime legacy, I traveled to Israel in the summer of 1989 to meet with three other former Turnatoria workers who lived just outside of Haifa.

At the appointed time, I asked the hotel desk clerk to dial a taxi. He said it would take about ten minutes to arrive. Instead of waiting, I walked straight outside. Within seconds, a cab pulled up to the curb, as if the driver had been expecting me. I got in and gave him the address. The driver asked me what I was doing in Israel.

"I'm working on a book."

"What about?"

"About a factory in Transnistria during the war."

"I was in Transnistria."

"You were? What did you do there?"

"I was the horse and wagon driver. I carted bodies to the cemetery."

"Then you must know the name Engineer Jagendorf."

"Is he alive?"

"No, he died almost twenty years ago. What can you tell me about him?"

He turned his head to face me for the first time and said, "If there is a *gan eden* [a garden of Eden], that is where you will find him." The cab driver was a godsend. Our seemingly serendipitous encounter tipped the scale in Jagendorf's favor.

Jagendorf's Foundry appeared in 1991 to critical acclaim. I had achieved my goal to see my name on the cover of a book, but it came at a price: overdosing on the Holocaust. For the next two years I wanted nothing to do with the subject.

— *marty* —

From Charleston to Atlanta

Finding myself in a new city with a new family, I turned my attention to earning a living.

I set up a consulting practice based on est training technology to support small business owners. I helped them clarify their commitments and create plans to fulfill them. This was an early version of what has now commonly known as "life coaching," in this case specifically for entrepreneurs.

I found Charleston to be very hospitable, but it became clear that moving to a larger city would be better for business. The logical choice was Atlanta, where I was still leading est seminars. After eleven years in Charleston, Marti too was ready for a change. We packed our belongings into a U-Haul van and made the six-hour drive to our new home, an apartment about five miles from downtown Atlanta. Andrea completed the remainder of first grade in a school that was a short walk from our home.

I set up shop on our dining room table, reaching out to Atlanta's many est graduates. Through participation in activities, workshops, and a host of events connected to the city's est center, my consulting business grew. Marti and I decided to have a child. One day, while going through the process of selecting a name, we decided to have lunch at one of our favorite restaurants. On the way, we spotted a street sign: Adina Drive. In Hebrew *adina* means delicate, fine, exquisite. We had found the perfect name.

In the spring of 1991, my good friend Tal, his wife Rachel, and their two-month-old son, Aviv, visited us from Israel. They told us how they had to shelter in the maternity ward to protect against a possible Iraqi missile attack. That evening Marti and I decided to have another child. Adam was born nine months later.

— *aron* —

Poland Beckons

In the winter of 1994, we were in Philadelphia to celebrate the bar mitzvah of a distant relative. I was at the pinnacle of my career as an editor, with a large and dedicated readership, and as a published author. When you feel that you have everything in hand, that's when life throws you a curveball.

As the party was winding down, two white-haired gentlemen approached me. They introduced themselves as *lantzmen*, countrymen, of my father. As if I needed proof, they pulled up their sleeves and displayed their Auschwitz numbers.

One of the brothers said intently, "We were recently in Bedzin and saw the building where your father's family lived. Are you planning to visit Poland anytime?" "Maybe someday," I replied. Sensing his disappointment in my lack of enthusiasm, I asked, "Where exactly is the building?" On the back of his business card he sketched a rough map of its location on Malachowska Street next to the railroad station. I tucked the card into my wallet.

The map was still in my pocket when a month later the vice president of Joseph Jacobs Advertising Agency phoned my office inviting me to join the first official Jewish press tour of Poland. "I'll go," I said, "but only if the itinerary includes Bedzin, my father's birthplace." It was a go. Bedzin was on the road to Auschwitz, one of the tour's planned destinations.

Since writing *Jagendorf's Foundry*, I had avoided the subject of the Holocaust. And since Pop's death, I had little inclination to look further into the tragic events of his past.

Yet here I was in the Polish capital participating in a somber ceremony marking the fifty-first anniversary of the Warsaw Ghetto Uprising. A military honor guard assisted various groups, government officials, and foreign dignitaries (among them the German and Israeli ambassadors) in laying a succession of floral wreaths at the base of sculptor Nathan Rapaport's monumental tribute to the heroic Jewish ghetto fighters.

Our group next visited the Umschlagplatz, the staging area for deportees from the Warsaw Ghetto. Its marble memorial wall bears the inscription: "Along this path of suffering over 300,000 Jews were driven in 1942–1943 to the gas chambers of the Nazi extermination camps."

Next we toured the thirty-acre Jewish cemetery on Okopowa Street containing a quarter million graves. A brick wall topped with barbed wire formed the backdrop of a monument dedicated to the memory of the 1.5 million Jewish children murdered by the Nazis. Photos of individual victims were embedded in a configuration of rocks at the base of the wall. At the time of our visit, fewer than 400 Jewish children lived in a nation that before the war had a Jewish population of more than 3.3 million.

At the Jewish community office in Warsaw, we were shown a set of volumes with hand-written messages left by newly liberated survivors in search of missing loved ones. I flipped through the pages of one and to my amazement found a message in Yiddish from Abram, my father's brother: "I am looking for information about the whereabouts of Wolf Manheimer of Bedzin." At that moment the press tour became personal.

— *marty* —

Unlikely Sunday School Teacher

Our family did not belong to a synagogue. Each year during the High Holy Days, we would drop in as guests at various houses of worship. After several years of nomadic observance, we joined The Temple, Atlanta's largest Reform synagogue, and enrolled Adam and Adina in its Sunday School.

I met with Senior Rabbi Alvin Sugarman to discuss how I might be able to contribute to the community based on my life experience. He suggested that I teach a sixth-grade Sunday school class that covered the Holocaust. I taught there for the five years that Adina and Adam attended Sunday school.

Despite my familiarity with the synagogue and warm relationship with Rabbi Sugarman, I couldn't shake off the discomfort, the underlying sadness I felt when sitting in the sanctuary and taking in the beautiful architecture, the stunning stained-glass windows, the ornate Torah ark. All I could think of was the many beautiful synagogues that had been destroyed by the Nazis and the families like mine who were annihilated. My association with Judaism was tethered to the history of Jewish persecution and suffering. I mostly kept these thoughts to myself.

When reminders of the Holocaust surfaced, I either "stuffed" the feeling or burst into tears for a few seconds. This surge of built-up emotion, like popping open a soda can, released the pressure just enough to restore my equilibrium.

— *aron* —

Next Stop Bedzin

The next stop of our press tour was Bedzin, Pop's birthplace.

As our van entered the city, the train station immediately came into view. I stepped out of the vehicle alone and approached the building marked X on the map handed to me at the bar mitzvah. I expected that moment to be highly emotional but felt nothing. After snapping a few photos, I walked to the kiosk in front of train station. Rose had asked me to bring home a piece of Bedzin that she could hold in her hand. I bought her a red comb.

Our guide informed us that there is a plaque somewhere on Malachowska Street memorializing the city's Jews who had perished in the

Holocaust. We eventually found the marker affixed to the exterior of a brick building. Unimpressive. The air smelled of factory waste. Respiratory diseases, we were told, are very common in this region known for coal mining and heavy industry.

As we continued walking along Malachowska Street, a thought popped into my head: What if Hitler had not rechanneled the course of history? My parents would have been married in Bedzin. I would have grown up in this place. Suddenly the imaginary number lifted from my arm. For the first time in my life, at age forty-seven, I was able to liberate myself from an identity that was not rightfully mine. What had happened to my parents during the war had not happened to me!

Before returning to the van, I asked our guide if we could visit the Jewish cemetery. He consented but had no idea of its location. None of the locals we asked had a clue as to its whereabouts. Then, from a distance, I saw a masonry archway inscribed with the Hebrew words for cemetery, *Beit Olam*. "It's just ahead," I said, but as we moved closer, the Hebrew letters suddenly vanished. My amazement was exceeded only by my embarrassment.

Having come this far, I waved the group toward the portal beneath the archway. We soon came upon a dark wooded slope dotted with long-abandoned Jewish gravestones. Everyone watched in silence as I wandered among the ancient Hebrew markers searching in vain for a "Manheimer."

When we returned to the van, my colleagues, notepads in hand, wanted to know my take on what just happened. At that moment, I didn't know what to make of the stunning graveyard discovery. Instead, I commented on the liberating moment when I imagined the Auschwitz tattoo flying off my arm. Only later did I understand the counter message of the cemetery experience: As a son of survivors, I am incapable of emotional disengagement from the horrors of the Holocaust. The call to witness is inescapable.

The Bedzin brothers corralling me at the bar mitzvah party, the unforeseen press tour invitation, the vanished *Beit Olam* letters—what was I, a rational person, to make of this curious chain of events? I am now convinced that my ancestral spirits had summoned me to the cemetery to hear their desperate plea: "Do not forget us!" Their message lies at the very heart of Judaism. From Sinai to Auschwitz, a Jew is obliged to remember and to bear witness, no matter how many generations removed.

Our press group sat in silence during the thirty-mile drive from Bedzin to Auschwitz. As we passed towering factory smokestacks, small farms, and long stretches of birch and pine forests, I tried to gauge my emotions. Would entering the notorious death camp unnerve me, or worse, numb me?

— *marty* —

Dreading Adam's Bar Mitzvah

As Adam approached the age of thirteen, I was happy that my only son, the last namesake of our family, would be experiencing this Jewish rite of passage and proud of how diligently he prepared for it. Yet I dreaded the thought of attending the ceremony because of my fraught relationship with Judaism and discomfort attending synagogue prayer services.

I didn't want to become such an emotional wreck that the event would be about me and not about Adam. Determined not to disappoint Adam and the rest of the family, six months before the bar mitzvah, I began to look for a psychologist. I needed someone who could help me remove the dark cloud that threatened to keep me from being fully present and experiencing the *naches*, the prideful joy, of this significant milestone.

— *aron* —

Auschwitz

On first impression, the Auschwitz-Birkenau State Museum resembled a theme park. Cars and buses crammed a parking lot the size of a football field. Inside the reception hall one could purchase snacks, guidebooks, postcards, and camera film. It was for good reason that a sign on the back wall reminded visitors that they are in a solemn place of remembrance and should act appropriately.

Our museum guide met us near the camp's main gate under the cynical sign *Arbeit Macht Frei*, Work Makes You Free. As we walked past the spot where an ensemble of prisoners had played music to supposedly lighten the mood in the camp, I noticed a door marked "Archives" and obtained permission to enter. The attendant handed me a request form. I listed a dozen names. She went into a backroom and soon returned with the results of her search: Pop's Auschwitz ID card. His prisoner number, 149719, matched the six digits tattooed on his arm. I learned from the document that on January 25, 1945, Pop was evacuated to Mauthausen, a concentration camp in Austria. Only two days later, Soviet troops liberated Auschwitz. For Pop, the worst was yet to come.

I rejoined the press group for a museum tour. The most chilling exhibition was a two-ton mound of hair sheared from as many as 140,000 victims, mostly women. Our guide explained that human hair was purchased by German firms for the manufacture of tailors' lining (haircloth). Nothing was wasted. Human ashes were utilized as fertilizer and landfill.

We next drove 1.86 miles to the adjacent camp, Birkenau, where as many as 100,000 prisoners were crowded into 300 rat-infested barracks. The vast majority of deportees who disembarked the cattle cars required no housing. After SS medical officer Josef Mengele selected them for death, they were marched from the railway ramp straight to the gas chambers.

At the edge of an ash container pond near the crematoria, our guide scraped the ground with her pen to unearth human bone fragments. I wondered if any of their DNA matched mine. We ended our tour by lighting six *yahrzeit* candles on the ruins of the gas chambers and reciting Kaddish.

I returned to Connecticut with the sense of liberation I had experienced in Bedzin still intact. In recognition of this transformation, I donated all but a few of my hundreds of Holocaust books to our temple library in honor of Pop.

Seeking a Psychologist's Help

I was fortunate to find a psychologist who could help me overcome my fear of being emotionally swept away at Adam's bar mitzvah. Dr. Avram Weiss and I had an instant rapport. He addressed not only my aversion to Jewish worship and to almost anything Holocaust related but also the post-traumatic stress of the Yom Kippur War that would ambush me from time to time. Each session with Dr. Weiss was cathartic. He allowed me to cry, cry, and cry some more as I unloaded years of pent-up sadness and despair. After several sessions, I felt emptied out, devoid of the energy to dredge up debilitating memories.

One of those memories revolved around the death of my friend Dubi, the battalion commander who was killed on the fourth day of the Yom Kippur War. I described to Dr. Weiss how Dubi was shot in the neck as he stepped off a half-track when our unit was attempting to recapture a Syrian fortification on the Golan Heights. Someone called out for help to remove Dubi's body from the vehicle. Though close by, I didn't respond. I couldn't bring myself to see or touch his body. The following day, I contacted our base office. His wife, who worked there, answered. I hung up. I did not want to be the one to answer her inevitable question: "Is Dubi all right?"

I had done Dubi wrong and didn't know how to release myself from the grip of guilt. For six years I held the strain and tension of this and other war memories in my throat. My neck felt like hardened leather. I could forcefully beat my fist against it and not feel a thing. In the course of my est training I was able to ask Dubi for forgiveness and to forgive myself. As my guilt eased, I felt a softening of the area around my throat. My sessions with Dr. Weiss allowed me to fully release this grip and partake in my son's bar mitzvah.

Adam chanted the Hebrew blessings and readings flawlessly and delivered a moving speech, dedicating it to the memory of family members we lost in the Holocaust. I then ascended the pulpit and with Adam at my side talked about what an extraordinary human being he had become and how much he took to heart the legacy of our survivor family. Through it all, only Marti was aware of the challenges I had confronted to be fully present at Adam's bar mitzvah.

It was the best day of my life.

— *aron* —

Staying the Course

A friend once asked me why Jews have been persecuted for so many centuries in so many places. At first I resented her question, thinking it implied that we somehow had it coming. Even worse, despite all my years as a Jewish educator and journalist, I had no answer.

This troubling question was on my mind when I asked Arthur Hertzberg—the renowned rabbi, author, professor, and public intellectual—if he would consider writing a book with me to answer some of the most perplexing questions about the Jewish historical experience. He thought for a moment about my proposal and said, "You mean like *The Italians* by Luigi Barzini." "Yes," I said, though I'd never heard of the book. He seemed intrigued by the idea and said, "I'll tell you what. If you can get us a publisher, I'm in." My literary agent and friend, Patti Breitman, sold Harper-Collins on *JEWS: The Essence and Character of a People*. The book appeared in 1998 and was eventually published in ten languages.

One chapter of the book addressed the persistence of antisemitism beginning with the archetypal Jew: Abraham. As the Torah teaches, God commands Abraham to leave the land of his birth. He becomes a sojourner. Wherever he pitches his tent, he remains an outsider. Jews have continued to follow in Abraham's footsteps, always refusing to give up their ancestral heritage and assimilate into the majority culture. This insistence on otherness has been met in every age with a furious backlash by those in the majority who want everyone to be like them, to affirm the correctness of their culture and beliefs. It is the price we pay to preserve our Jewishness.

Rabbi Hertzberg taught me that as long as the Jewish people exist, antisemitism will persist. In more tolerant times and places, when Jews were given the opportunity to take the exit door, only the most ardent clung to the traditions of their ancestors. The Manheimer and Yura families have chosen to stay the course and endure the hatred and violence of those bent on annihilating *Am Yisrael*, the Jewish people.

— *marty* —

A Generation Passes

Wanting our children to develop relationships with their grandmother, Buba Sophie, as well as Aunt Aga and Uncle Lolek, we traveled to Los Angeles regularly when they were young. I will always remember the twinkle in Buba's eyes as she played with her *einicklech*, grandkids. The same was true for Uncle Lolek, who was not known for mushiness. To this day our kids fondly recall those visits.

After my mother's second husband, Max, died in 1994, she lived alone, just as she had after my father passed away twenty-two years earlier. Though they did not drive, Aunt Aga and Uncle Lolek were self-sufficient. They walked to and from the grocery store, which probably contributed to their longevity, and took buses for visits to the doctor.

Max's children looked in on my mother for about three years, until Marti and I moved her to Atlanta to be closer to us. We set her up in an independent living facility and moved her to managed care when she required more attention. We visited her frequently and brought her to our home every week to celebrate Shabbat. When she began to show signs of dementia, our kids were very patient with her.

I visited my aunt and uncle in LA about once a year. They remained strong and active but missed my mother and the rest of our family. Uncle Lolek entered hospice care in January 2001. I sat at his bedside, thanked him for being so integral to my life, told him I loved him, and said goodbye. He passed the following week at age ninety-five. I returned to LA to arrange his funeral.

We moved Aunt Aga to Atlanta, where she took a room in the managed-care home where my mother lived. I hadn't told my mother of Lolek's passing. Her dementia was advancing and we didn't want to say anything that might upset her. Sound familiar? When I brought Aga into my mother's room after a separation of a few years, my mother didn't recognize her at first, but they seemed to connect after a couple of days. I don't know whether my mother was able to understand that Lolek was "no more," as Aga said of people who had died.

My mother would always express delight at seeing me. She did the same with Marti and the kids, although we weren't sure whether she actually recognized us or if this was simply her natural inclination. When I'd leave the room for a few moments, she'd be all smiles upon my return, as if she hadn't seen me in a week.

Marti and I saw Buba and Aunt Aga a few times a week either at the care home or at our house. When Buba needed her diaper changed, something I could just not bring myself to do, Marti did so lovingly, as if she were her own mother. After Buba had a hip replaced, she began to decline rapidly and entered hospice care in mid-July of 2001. A week later, I received a call informing me that she had passed peacefully in the night. She was ninety-two. As I hurriedly prepared to go to the hospice center, Marti turned to me and said gently, "She's gone. There's no reason to hurry."

An hour later, I sat alone at my mother's side, finding the quiet time with her consoling. I expressed my love for her and kissed her forehead. She had been a loving mother and a good person.

I honored her wish to be buried beside my father. The following day I was on an El Al flight to Israel with the casket stored in the plane's cargo hold. My Israeli friend, Tal, who had been the best man at our Jewish wedding, picked me up at Lod Airport and I spent the night at his home near Tel Aviv. In the morning we drove to the Kfar Saba cemetery. I was greeted by my cousins Zvi and Bronka and their families before being ushered by a staff person into a small building to confirm the identity of the deceased. A white sheet was pulled down uncovering my mother's face. I nodded.

The mourners walked down a grass path toward the place of burial. We stood around the freshly dug earth and watched as her body, wrapped in a white sheet according to Jewish custom, was lowered. I recited Kaddish in the very spot I had for my father almost thirty years earlier. A rabbi chanted the El Maleh Rachamim, God full of passion, a plea that the soul of the departed be granted proper rest. I remained at the gravesite for a few minutes after the others left. And that was it. I returned to Atlanta a few days later.

Aunt Aga was able to witness the passing of loved ones with a quiet sense of dignity and resilience. She never expressed bitterness or anger, despite the horrors and obstacles she had endured. She adored our children, always carrying a little something for them, like a chocolate bar she had won at bingo. Her eyes would light up, twinkle, in the presence of our kids.

As Aunt Aga began to weaken, she did not fear death. She understood when we brought her to hospice that this was the next step. Aunt Aga passed away on October 7, 2007, at age ninety-seven. I accompanied her body back to Los Angeles, where she was buried next to Lolek.

Perhaps because I was older when my aunt died, I could better appreciate her extraordinary qualities. At times I miss her more than I miss my parents.

— *aron* —

The Death March Dybbuk

In the spring of 1995, Ma received a letter from Svatopluk Vokurka, mayor of Volary in the Czech Republic. He wrote: "You are connected to our town through your experience at the end of World War II. We will remember events that happened here fifty years ago. We invite you to celebrate this liberation with us from May 3 to 5."

Ma had no intention of ever returning to Europe, but after Rose and I said we would accompany her, she accepted the invitation. We wanted to stand on the very ground where she had made her daring escape on May 5, 1945, after having been forced to trudge 350 miles under the most inhumane conditions imaginable.

While our parents shared few details of their Holocaust experience, the story Ma told us of her final day of captivity was an exception:

> When the SS guards saw that I was too exhausted to continue the march, they forced me and about twenty-five other girls onto the back of an open truck. We all knew that they were going to kill us in a forest. After we rode for a short time, an American fighter plane flew overhead and started shooting at us.
>
> The guard sitting beside me—a pregnant SS woman—was hit

in the stomach. I didn't even get a scratch. In the confusion, I said to Tzipora, the woman who had shared a bed and blanket with me in Grünberg, "Now is the time to get away." She was too afraid to move. I somehow found the strength to pull her off the truck.

We crossed a field that led to a narrow river. We didn't know how to swim but kept going, terrified that the guards were coming after us. The water came up to our necks. We got across and hid in a barn under a stack of hay. When we saw a woman enter, we shook the hay to get her attention. She screamed in German, "Holy Jesus, what do you want here?" We told her we are Jews and asked for a drink of water. She said, "It is not safe for you to remain here" and pointed us to a wooded hill nearby. We did as she said. After dark, she brought us milk.

The next day a group of liberated French slave laborers found us and gave us some food to eat. They then carried us on crisscrossed arms back to the road. I weighed less than seventy pounds. A Red Cross ambulance took us to the hospital in Volary. Our American military doctors told us that the war was over. The Germans had surrendered.

Not all the women remaining on the truck had been shot on the spot as Ma believed. Jadzia Goldblum Kichler, one of the survivors who traveled to Volary from Toronto for the reunion, recounted what had happened to her and the other women after the truck came under attack.

All three SS women were hit, but not a single Jewish girl. One of them was killed on the spot and the two injured were evacuated to the hospital in Volary. The SS men locked us in a stable near the road. In the morning they returned and ordered us to walk into the woods, promising to give us food. We refused to move, fearing we'd be killed. They selected eight girls and shot them against a row of large rocks at the edge of a field. The rest of us were then forced to climb up a steep hill, where fourteen more were shot dead, one after the other. Only three of us remained alive when the killing stopped. The killers put on civilian clothes and one of them said, "You are free to go." We stood still until they threw down their weapons and walked away.

Ninety-five death march victims are buried in a dedicated cemetery in the heart of Volary. In a special ceremony, our group placed flowers beneath a twelve-foot-high memorial sculpture of a female form rising above this meticulously maintained burial ground. On behalf of the town's 4,000 inhabitants, the mayor pledged "to always take care of these graves as a duty of honor."

In the town's movie theater, Mayor Vokurka presented each of the twenty-four survivors with a commemorative silver coin, a statuette modeled on the cemetery sculpture, and a red rose. School children gave each of the women a craft they had made for the occasion. Speeches, concerts, a folk-dance performance, a banquet, a parade, and the largest fireworks display in the town's history topped off the three days of festivities honoring these heroic women who personified triumph over Nazi tyranny. Of the more than 1,000 women on the death march, only one in five lived to bear witness.

In our hotel room on the final night of the trip, Ma let down her guard and described in detail how each camp along the death march was more dehumanizing than the last. Neither Rose nor I could sleep that night. Rose came to my room and we just hugged each other. The next morning, as our bus was about to leave for the airport, Ma said to me, "By taking you here, I accomplished a big step. This is the greatest gift I could have given to you and your sister. You now have a better understanding of what is important in life and what is not."

When we returned to Los Angeles, Rose fell into a serious depression, burdened by what she had learned about the horrors our mother had endured. Ma, on the other hand, had never been so serene and content with her life. By changing the narrative from one of suffering and humiliation to one of heroism and celebrity, Mayor Vokurka had liberated Ma from the death march dybbuk, the malevolent spirit that had haunted her for half a century.

— *marty* —
Bad Timing

I invested a substantial amount of our family savings in a start-up internet company that quickly failed. Not only was the company undercapitalized, but the timing was bad, just prior to the Great Recession of 2008. Our bank balance was insufficient to cover our anticipated expenses for the coming year.

As a son of survivors, I have always had a lingering concern about the possibility of sudden loss, but that did not deter me from taking business risks. Some paid off; this one didn't. Marti, who has always trusted me to manage our money, did not blame me for the sudden precariousness of our financial state. We shared the belief that through honest introspection and committed action a new door would open to us. We were unwilling to be victims of the circumstance.

Marti had been practicing yoga for many years and eventually became a certified yoga teacher. At first, I did not share her enthusiasm. A yoga class I had taken twenty-five years earlier on a hot and humid summer day in Charleston left me feeling clumsy, inept, disoriented, and overheated.

I resisted giving yoga a second chance before finally agreeing to join a class Marti was teaching at a local health center. I stepped into the class hesitatingly, placing my mat at the rear of the room. Marti's mastery as a teacher eased me through the flowing sequence of vinyasa. My attendance was sporadic at first, but after taking the class for several weeks, the tightness in my body began to loosen. I told Marti that yoga was doing me some good.

What had not changed was our money woes. Then on Christmas Eve 2008, our adult children sitting with us around the kitchen counter, Marti turned to me and asked in her characteristically assertive yet supportive tone, "What do you want to do next"? I looked at her and said, "Let's open a yoga center together."

Our next move was to get in touch with the power of commitment. If you truly commit to a purpose, all kinds of things can begin to fall into place to support you on your journey.

Still, there was no guarantee that starting a new business in the midst of a recession would be a wise move. What convinced me to proceed was my ability to create and sustain a supportive structure for projects, coupled with my confidence in Marti's can-do spirit and tenacity. Add to that her extraordinary skill and charisma as a yoga teacher. If I were choosing up sides, I'd always want Marti on my team.

I registered for a 200-hour yoga teacher training course in Atlanta, and we began searching for a location. We chose a building that had been a supermarket in a small strip mall. As the daughter of a builder, Marti had a knack for efficient spatial design, which enabled us to build out a state-of-the-art 2,500-square-foot studio on a slim budget. We signed a five-year commercial lease and celebrated the grand opening of Vista Yoga on Saturday, November 14, 2009.

Our bet paid off. Five years later, we renewed our lease and built out the adjacent space, adding a second studio, another massage room, and a teaching kitchen where we conduct healthy food preparation classes.

Although I was unaware of the profound and ongoing impact that yoga would continue to have on my life, my practice had become integral to keeping me healthy and physically fit, as well as emotionally and mentally resilient.

— *aron* —

Reconnecting with Marty

On Christmas Eve 2016, I got a frantic call from my daughter, Mimi. She was stranded at the Atlanta airport with her husband, Wes, and toddler son, Eddie. Heavy rains had caused the cancellation of all connecting flights. Mimi asked me what to do. I told her that my old friend Marty Yura lived in Atlanta and gave her his phone number.

I had no doubt that Marty would come to their rescue. The following day, Mimi called to tell us how warmly the Yura family had embraced them. She then said, "The atmosphere of their home is just like yours, from the art on the walls to the *tchotchkes,* knickknacks. I don't understand why you guys don't get together sometime."

I suppose if Marty and I hadn't lived so far apart, we would have gotten together more often. With distance came misunderstandings, at least on my part. I was under the impression that Marty had gotten himself ensnared in est, which I thought of as a cult. Unaware that his wife had converted to Judaism and that he had taught religious school at Atlanta's largest Reform temple, I was under the false impression that Marty had abandoned all things Jewish.

When we would call each other on our birthdays, Marty sometimes talked about his work, but I could never quite grasp what he did for a living. I pictured him going from one startup to another, the type of person our parents would describe disapprovingly as a *luftmensch*, a man floating in air. As it turned out, all my assumptions about Marty and his life in Atlanta were wrong. Though I did not know it, Marty and I still had a great deal in common beyond memories of days gone by.

I took to heart Mimi's urging that Marty and I get together.

— *marty* —
Reconnecting with Aron

When Mimi called me from the Atlanta airport and explained their predicament, we were about to head out to the home of Adina and her husband, Rafael, for a holiday dinner. Mimi, Wes, and Eddie were immediately welcomed and included in our family festivities. They fit right in. Mimi and Adina were about the same age and instantly found rapport. It felt as if I had known Mimi forever. Her presence made me feel closer to Aron.

Mimi and her family were the catalyst that prompted Aron and me to revive our relationship. Neither of us had a good answer to Mimi's question of why we didn't get together sometime.

The only time that Aron and I had seen one another since Israel 1973 was when he came to Atlanta for a Union for Reform Judaism board meeting. We met for breakfast at his hotel. Although we were happy to spend some time together, I was left with an odd impression. Experiencing some financial challenges at the time, I didn't find it very endearing to hear him talk about how well his career at the magazine and family business were going. I wrote Aron off as being in a different orbit than me. I also felt that he had found his path while I was still grappling to find mine. I hadn't let any of these feelings disrupt our custom of annual birthday calls, which always gave me a bit of a lift.

I think both our lives had "gotten in the way" as we attended to what was in front of us as husbands, fathers, grandfathers, and breadwinners. Mimi's visit resulted in a return to the brother-like relationship that Aron and I had enjoyed decades earlier. Our seemingly serendipitous reunion allowed us to once again become the closest of friends.

— *aron* —

Closing the Time Gap

During the spring of 2017, Marty told me that he and his wife would be coming to Manhattan for a short stay and asked if Judy and I might be able to get together with them. We welcomed the opportunity and took a train to the city. Marty was waiting for us at his hotel. He looked very different from how I had pictured him. What stood out most to me was how much his face had become a reincarnation of his father's. He was also significantly slimmer and held himself straighter than before. I assumed there was a yoga connection. He confirmed it, saying that Marti, who would soon be joining us at a Midtown patisserie, minded his posture.

Marty and I had fun recalling and sharing some of our adventures together, quickly closing the time gap and reaffirming our bond of friendship. Judy and Marti also had much in common, and all of us left the table promising to meet again soon.

— *marty* —

Surprise!

Rose and I spoke the week before Aron's seventieth birthday. She said, "Wouldn't it be awesome if you showed up in Los Angeles and surprised him?" I thought it was a great idea, especially since I had told Aron that I would not be able to get away at that time. On the morning of January 28, 2018, the day before the party, I rang the doorbell of his mother's house and watched Aron's jaw drop and eyes light up as he opened the door and saw me standing there.

Several of Aron's friends from different periods of his life attended the party at Rose and Bitzy's house. After expressing gratitude to his mother and sister, Aron talked about how each of his friends in the room had been a major influence in his life. No one could have felt closer to Aron than I did that day. A new chapter had opened in our lives.

chapter five

Bearing Witness

Uncovering Our Parents' Pasts

— aron —

Out of the Dark

Brothers again, Marty and I began to communicate more often. Though we didn't talk about our common Holocaust legacy, I had the feeling that the subject was lurking in the background. Perhaps Marty was thinking that I could somehow help him sort out some unresolved issues. I did have an abundance of experience with the subject as a journalist and author, so it came as no surprise when Marty eventually confided in me about the difficulties he had controlling his emotions. He cried whenever we touched on a painful episode, like when he told me about the tragic fate of his father's first family.

As one who had learned to intellectualize the subject, I was able to be a sounding board for Marty with little emotional interference on my end. Believing that it was better to know what happened than to be kept in the dark, I encouraged Marty to confront his demons head on.

— *marty* —
The Dude and the Zen Master

Whenever someone asked me if I ever considered going to Poland, my answer was always an emphatic NO. Any visit to Poland, to a concentration camp memorial site, or to my parents' hometowns had always been off the table. Why would I want to go to Auschwitz? It would be like sticking my finger in a hot light socket. Then I read *The Dude and the Zen Master* (2017), a book co-authored by Zen master Bernie Glassman and actor Jeff Bridges, who had played the role of "the Dude" in the movie, *The Big Lebowski*.

In the book, the authors riff about life while spending a week together at Bridges's ranch. At one point, Bernie mentions the Zen Peacemakers, an organization he founded that holds an annual five-day immersion retreat at the site of Auschwitz-Birkenau. Participants are asked to leave behind their assumptions about what they think they know, to bear witness, and to take loving action in pursuit of peace. In the book, Bernie defines peace as realizing the interconnectedness and wholeness of life and points out that in Hebrew the root of *shalom*, peace, is *shalem*, which means whole.

I knew instinctively that this was an opportunity not to miss. I thought of a swimmer about to spring from a high diving board, suspended in fear and trepidation. The Zen Peacemakers presented an opening, an opportunity for me to confront the nagging and unrelenting questions that had haunted me throughout my life: What might it have been like to be in the very place where so many unimaginable atrocities had been perpetrated, where my father had been imprisoned and his family murdered?

After reading accounts of past program participants, I phoned the Zen Peacemakers office. Rami Efal, the executive director at the time, "got me." He understood my concerns. I felt a sense of safety in knowing that I would not be bearing witness alone, but in the company of a group of people with a shared purpose to do good.

Before signing up, I asked Aron if he'd be interested in joining me. He explained that he had already visited the former death camp three times and had no desire to go again. Aron was unfamiliar with the Zen

Peacemakers but encouraged me to go for it. Marti was supportive as well, hoping that the trip would free me from the nagging question of whether I could have survived a concentration camp, as my father had.

The Zen Peacemakers was a crack from which the light of possibility peeked through. My personal liberation from the emotional grip of this not-so-distant past had begun, even before I set foot in Auschwitz.

— *aron* —

Unfinished Business

I was impressed that Marty had found the courage to sign on to the Zen Peacemakers. Though I had declined to accompany him, I was about to embark on a journey of my own. The time had come to pull back the curtain on my own family's Holocaust experiences beyond Ma's jumping from the truck and Pop's jumping from the train. There was so much more about which I knew next to nothing.

The best source of information about what happened to Pop's family in Bedzin had been collecting dust in my home library for almost fifty years. It was a 1961 memoir that Pop's brother, Abram, had published in Argentina titled *Condenado 133649* (Condemned 133649), under the pen name Alberto Mann. The cover shows an arm tattooed with Abram's Auschwitz prisoner number, 133649, grasping barbed wire against the background of a guard tower. When I visited Buenos Aires in January of 1968 to represent our family at the wedding of his daughter, Raquel, Abram handed me a copy of the book, inscribed, "*A mi querido sobrino Aron con carino*" (To my dear nephew Aron with affection)."

Before the wedding, Abram and I spent a few hours at his kitchen table translating the first few pages of his book from Spanish into Yiddish. He expected me to translate the entire book into English when I got home. Instead, I placed it on a bookshelf with other survivor memoirs, and there it sat.

Abram laughed easily and liked to have a good time. Beneath the surface, he was a man wracked with pain and sorrow. I avoided asking Abram about the past, partly because I didn't want to get mired in some disagreeable family politics.

The rift between the two branches of our family dated back to their time together in the Feldafing Displaced Persons Camp. Apparently, my parents had not approved of Abram's choice of Clara as his bride. Her revenge was to drive a wedge between the two brothers and our families. For years, Clara disposed of Pop's letters before Abram could see them. For her part, Ma often complained to me and Rose about how badly Clara had treated her in the Feldafing DP Camp.

Though Abram and his family visited us once in Cleveland in the 1950s and later in Los Angeles, old resentments persisted. Abram intimated that Pop was somehow responsible for the death of their brother, Piniek, for having left him behind on the train after Pop jumped. It had always been my understanding, though I don't recall who told me, that Pop threw himself from the train in a moment of grief and desperation after Piniek died in his arms.

In 1993, Raquel's son, Ariel, came to visit us in Connecticut. He was on a mission of reconciliation, but it would take several more years for Clara's influence to wane. For me, the low point was not learning until after his funeral that Abram had died from cancer on August 8, 2000.

I took the news hard and vented in a letter to Raquel, which I don't think was ever mailed:

> It has been a week now since Ariel phoned me with the sad news. I feel the loss of Abram very deeply, as much, in some ways, as the death of my own father. Mixed with the sadness is a feeling of sorrow that I was not allowed the opportunity to say goodbye to him. Surely there must be a statute of limitations on family feuds....
>
> Let us bridge the distance that separates us in miles with a tearful embrace of recovered love. Raquel, I know you feel the same way; otherwise, I don't think you would have asked Ariel to phone me. I know that Clara is determined to cut the thread that still binds our family, and I understand that as a dutiful daughter you want to honor her wishes. But do you really think it is fair to

punish the children for the sins of the parents? I do not.... I have always loved Abram, and my heart is broken.

Three months later, I wrote a letter to Abram, or should I say to his spirit, concerning some unfinished business:

> Dear Abram, I write this letter to you while your soul is still in the realm somewhere between this world and *olam haba*, the world to come. And I know in my heart that you will receive this message, for it concerns some unfinished business.
>
> When Ariel phoned me after your funeral, I felt a double loss—the grief of losing a beloved uncle and the hurt of having been denied a final farewell. I do not blame you. What good is it at this point to apportion blame? But it is never too late for a *cheshbon ha-nefesh*, an accounting of the soul, and in this regard I can only judge myself.
>
> Can I honestly say that my actions faithfully reflected my true feelings for you? Regretfully, I waited for you to reach out to me, knowing that you could do so only by incurring the wrath of your wife. Perhaps if I had come to Buenos Aires or arranged to see you in Miami, things might have been different ...
>
> But even as I write these words of reconciliation, it is not within my power to forgive you for the pain you have so unjustly caused my mother. Why did you cut her off after the death of my father, as if she no longer existed? If it is possible to do *teshuvah*, atone, where you now reside, then cleanse your soul and petition her forgiveness. I believe she will forgive you because she has always loved you as a brother. And if you find it in your heart to do the right thing, the angels in heaven will dance a tango in your honor.

In the aftermath of Abram's death, Raquel and her family started coming to our family celebrations in America, and we in turn attended their *simchas* in Argentina. When Raquel's daughter, Debi, saw me for the first time at the arrivals terminal at the JFK airport, she cried. I asked her why. She said, "I look at you and I see Abram."

On one of our visits to Buenos Aires, Clara told me that she forgives my mother and wants peace in the family. I shared her wishes with Ma, but the two women never reconnected. Clara died in Buenos Aires on September 5, 2014, at the age of ninety-one. When Marty and I decided to write our memoir, I asked Ariel if he would be willing to translate *Condenado 133649* into English for me. Having been emotionally overwhelmed when he read it years earlier, Ariel was initially reluctant to take it on. He told me that Abram talked about the Holocaust to a fault.

> Every day when I came home from high school and walked up the stairs to our apartment, which was next to his, I would say, "Hi. How are you?" and he would start talking about the Shoah. I couldn't stop myself from crying, so intense was his grief and suffering. I would always say, "Let's talk about something else."
>
> He could also be fun. Often when I came into his apartment, he was playing the piano and singing. We used to play cards. I had the greatest relationship with my grandfather. He told me that someday I would finish what he couldn't. I now understand that to mean that he wanted me to restore peace to the Manheimer family.

Ariel had fulfilled Abram's final wish and in that spirit agreed to translate the book. As Marty was seeking answers on his Zen Peacemakers retreat in Poland, it was time for me to learn the contents of Abram's memoir and find some answers of my own.

— *marty* —

What Would I Have Done?

My plane landed in Krakow on a Friday night, November 3, 2017. I had always imagined Poland as a dark and dreary place, absent any color. I was surprised the next morning to see families happily strolling the streets under the bright blue sky of this architecturally pleasing city. I spent most of the weekend exploring and enjoying Krakow's coffeehouses and eateries, public parks, and the castle across the street from my hotel.

On Monday morning I met some of the more than seventy Zen Peacemakers participants in front of our hotel as we prepared to board buses to our destination. They varied in age, religious affiliation, and nationality. Some were descendants of victims, others of perpetrators. Some were clear about their intentions, others not so much. Some were first-timers, others returnees. Over the five-day retreat, I learned from several German participants that they had unrepentant Nazis in their families, a subject shrouded in secrecy. Our shared legacies of trauma created an odd closeness between us.

After an hour-long bus drive through picturesque countryside, our group arrived at Auschwitz-Birkenau. Our first stop was a hall with several rows of seats. We viewed a documentary showing the Red Army liberating the camp. Nothing was censored. It was shocking to view the vast number of stacked naked corpses, mouths agape. Never had I seen images of so many child prisoners, their eyes looking listlessly into the camera's lens. I thought, "How could they have survived? How could they ever be 'normal?'"

We gathered at the infamous *Arbeit Macht Frei* sign at the entrance of Auschwitz and toured several barracks. Some housed museum-like displays of stacks of suitcases, shoes, prosthetic devices, and other plundered property. Other barracks were kept intact, allowing visitors to view rows of multilevel wooden bunks. The kapos, brutal enforcers who served the Nazis by beating, punishing, and killing fellow prisoners, had separate barracks, better conditions, and received payment for their services.

We were shown torture rooms, some of them coffin-sized chambers with no space to move. Outside we stood before the "killing wall," where prisoners were lined up and shot or hung from posts. I was reminded of a scene described in a book by Auschwitz survivor Primo Levi. A fellow prisoner asks him rhetorically, "Where is God?" Levi points to a five-year-old boy who had just been hung to death. Two of my grandsons are that boy's age now. As I write this, I'm sobbing, feeling like a wire brush is moving across my heart.

We were shown an early version of a gas chamber, then a crematorium where bodies were turned to ash for disposal. An electrified fence surrounded the camp perimeter. How easy it would have been for prisoners to throw themselves against the barrier and end it all. Had I been a prisoner here, would I have flung myself onto the fence? Would I have been able to survive? Perhaps asking myself these lingering questions was a way of putting myself in my father's place when he was confronted daily with life and death choices as a captive here.

My first day was certainly trying, but not overwhelming. I managed not to "lose it."

— *aron* —

Rescue in Bedzin

I had never given much thought to what the Nazi occupation of Bedzin must have been like for Pop's family. All I knew was that his engagement party had to be called off because my mother was sent off to a concentration camp. Abram's memoir transported me to that time, leaving little room for mystery.

I didn't know that the Nazi selection process in Bedzin began a year before the last of its 27,000 Jews were sent to Auschwitz in August of 1943. Abram describes how signs were posted directing all Jews to appear on the fields of the city's sports clubs. The Manheimers reported to the Hakoach soccer field, where they were forced to sit all day long on the grass, surrounded by soldiers. When the stadium was filled to capacity, the Germans paraded the Jews past several Gestapo officers. "As we passed," Abram writes, "they assigned everyone a number and lined us up accordingly. Those fortunate enough to be included in group 1 were considered 'fit to work.' Those in group 3 were condemned to the crematoria in Auschwitz, and those in group 2 were held in reserve in case the death quota was not filled."

Abram's mother was assigned to group 3 and his father to group 2. "At two in the morning," he writes, "our father came home, but our mother remained a condemned prisoner." At dawn, Abram went on a reconnaissance mission to find his mother's precise location. From the street he scouted a five-story building where most of the detainees were held. He saw his mother peering down at him from an upper floor window but couldn't make out what she was saying.

The Manheimer brothers devised a high-risk rescue plan. Posing as repairmen, Abram and Piniek would enter the adjacent building. If they were lucky, they would be able to reach the top floor and bore a hole in the wall wide enough for them to enter the building where their mother was being held—all this without being caught.

Everything went according to plan. They broke through the wall, descended the stairs, and went from room to room until they found her. What they didn't expect was her state of mind. "She was sitting on the ground, deep in thought," writes Abram.

> Her gaunt face, flooded with tears, revealed the emotional torture to which she had been subjected. We feared that she would come out of her trance-like state and cry out, alerting the guards. Seeing us approach, she shook her head in resignation, thinking that we too were going to share her sad fate. We communicated to her in gestures and whispers that we had come to rescue her. She resisted. With tenderness we impelled her to follow us. Step by step, we slowly climbed the stairs until we reached the opening to the neighboring building.

It must have been a slow, agonizing rescue, knowing that at any moment they could be found out. And yet, their audacious plan succeeded. It could not have come sooner. That very afternoon the detainees held in those buildings were "resettled in the East," never to return.

Birkenau

We spent the following four days in Birkenau, which we were told had been constructed to expand the killing capacity of Auschwitz. It encompassed

300 buildings, mostly barracks, and four gas chambers and crematoria. Several of the barracks had been destroyed, but many remained. Fortified barbed wire fences surrounded the perimeter along with tall guard towers evenly spaced.

Each morning we walked about 200 yards into the camp and spent part of the day sitting in silence at the point where the railroad tracks ended. It was here that from 1942 to 1945 rail cars packed to the brim arrived almost daily with thousands of deportees from across Europe. The new arrivals were "selected" for slave labor, "medical" experimentation, or immediate extermination. About ninety percent of those arriving, mainly older people and women with children, were marched directly to the gas chambers.

At the site of one almost-demolished gas chamber we followed the path where those selected for extermination were lined up before walking down some stairs to a long hall-like room to prepare for "a shower." They were instructed to disrobe and to hang their clothing onto wall hooks. They were then crowded into a chamber with shower head devices in the ceiling. Heavy wooden doors locked them inside and poison gas was released. Within minutes everyone was dead. The doors were then opened and the bodies removed by a unit of Jewish prisoners called *Sonderkommandos*. Other prisoners then extracted gold fillings from the victims' teeth and sheared off their hair for industrial use in Germany. The final step in this gruesome process was to cart the corpses to the crematoria for incineration. In this way, the Germans systematically murdered more than a million people.

At the site of one of the gas chambers, a rabbi led our group in the reciting of Kaddish. Other clergy were present as well. We stood for a moment of silence. Too much to comprehend. No words. No commentary going on in my head.

Every morning and afternoon our group would sit on the ground in a circle. We took turns reading out loud the names of victims. It was a way of connecting with the countless souls who would forever inhabit this place.

One evening, during a group meeting to share our experiences, it struck me that my then two-and-a-half-year-old granddaughter, Emilia, was about the same age as my father's younger daughter Ruthie when she was murdered here. At that moment, the lists of victims' names and photos we had been seeing merged in my mind with the image of my own grandchild. In this moment I nearly "lost it."

— *aron* —

The Bunker

The daring rescue of my grandmother belied the characterization that Jews went like sheep to the slaughter. The Manheimer brothers continued their resistance by constructing a secret room under their building on Malachowska Street. The decision came after they received news that the Nazis had put down the Warsaw Ghetto Uprising in May of 1943 and deported the surviving ghetto residents to concentration camps. "In that final combat," writes Abram, "perhaps with weapons in hand, my sister and brother-in-law died."

He was referring to his oldest sister, Raquel, and her husband, identified by Abram as "Cimbalista—a man with a solid cultural background and good economic position." The couple had moved in 1936 to Katowice, a city seven miles south of Bedzin. Three years later, after the Germans invaded Poland, they sought refuge in Warsaw, where, Abram writes, "they hoped to find salvation but found only death." Their two-year-old son, Simon (Shimeleh), perished with them.

Construction of the bunker took ten weeks to complete. It was furnished with nine narrow wooden cots, three cabinets attached to the walls, a table, benches, a water tank, batteries, candles, and a half-year's supply of food and water. The family stayed in the bunker throughout the night, while one of the brothers stood guard at a top floor window of the building.

One evening just before sunset, Piniek spotted Nazis raiding houses nearby. Within minutes the Manheimers took refuge in the bunker and sealed off the entrance. "The silence," writes Abram, "was broken only by the beating of our hearts, our breathing, and the slight snoring of my sister

Tonia's little son, who was just eighteen months old. Tonia fed the boy two sleeping pills, as she did every time there was a raid. At dawn we heard the sound of approaching boots, louder and louder. Failing to find us, they began to bang on the floors and walls. The noise woke up the baby. He began to cry. Our efforts to silence him failed."

Though the Germans gave up the search, Tonia insisted on leaving the bunker with her son to spare the rest of us. We all pleaded with her not to sacrifice herself and her son. She rejected the idea that we all share the same fate. Tonia went away the next morning and was never heard from again. "Her farewell kiss," writes Abram, "still burns on my forehead."

The brothers checked on their sister Pola, who was eight months pregnant and lived with her husband two blocks away. Finding the house in shambles, they went to see Alfred Rossner, head of a textile factory where Pola's husband worked. Rossner obtained permission to exempt him from deportation to Auschwitz on the grounds that he was a skilled worker. "He refused the reprieve," writes Abram, "preferring to share the fate of his wife and their unborn child."

The Nazis intensified their raids on the remaining hiding places in Bedzin. The Manheimer bunker, now overcrowded because they didn't have the heart to turn away desperate people, was discovered on the third day of the action. Designed for nine people, the number had grown to twenty-three. One of the men in the bunker had a mental breakdown. His wife began to sob. Before she could be quieted down, a machine gun blast tore through one of the bunker walls, fatally wounding those closest to it. Then came the command: "*Aus, verfluchte Juden*" (Out, cursed Jews). One by one we slowly emerged to the amazement of the Nazis, who had come close but never located the secret trap door. The captives were taken to a plaza crowded with Jews awaiting the order to march to the railway station.

Abram describes as "Dante-esque" what followed:

> A huge truck carrying empty sacks arrived. The Nazis corralled the children like animals and stuffed them into the sacks. The bundles were then stacked in a truck to be transported to a waiting train that would take us all to the gates of eternity. The locomotive's

thick black smoke foreshadowed what we would soon see spewing from the chimneys of Auschwitz.

The rescue of my grandmother, the bunker, the self-sacrifice of Tonia and Pola's husband in acts of pure love gave me a profound appreciation of the courage and nobility of family members who perished in the Holocaust. The more I learned about each of them, the deeper was my sorrow and my desire to preserve their memories.

Bye Bye Birkenau

After Aron told me that he had found information about his father at the Auschwitz archives, I contacted them prior to the Zen Peacemakers retreat, inquiring if they had any prisoner records on Jerry Yura. I received a positive response. During a break on the fourth day of the retreat, I met with the chief archivist. He invited me to join him at a conference table in his office and set down a folder between us. He handed me the intake document my father had signed upon arrival at the camp.

> Name: Jura, Icek Israel [The Nazis routinely added the name "Israel" to names of Jewish males and "Sarah" to names of females]
> Prisoner number: 175073
> Born: October 17, 1904 in Proszowice, Poland, Residence: Bendsburg [Bedzin]
> Race: Jude [Jew]
> Arrested: March 3, 1944 in Katowice, Poland
> Arrived at Auschwitz: March 14, 1944
> Married to Gitla Borzjkowski, 2 children
> Nationality: Polish
> Parents: Herszel and Chaia
> Occupation: Public servant
> Physical Characteristics: Strong Build
> Languages: Polish, German

Criminal History: None. No arrests for political activity.

That was followed by several lists with "1 mark" appearing next to my father's name. The archivist explained that my father had received a stipend for working as a "scribe," one who gives camp officials a daily tally of prisoners in each barrack. Disparities in daily prisoner counts indicated how many had died from one day to the next. I immediately understood that the stipend enabled my father to purchase the life-saving food he smuggled to his brother Moshe's daughter, Helen, in the women's section of the camp. (Helen survived and married Richard, also a survivor. They ended up in Detroit after the war and had two daughters. Helen and her family absolutely adored my father, treating him as the family patriarch.)

That evening at sundown our group returned to Birkenau. I experienced a shuddering moment in one of the barracks. We were sitting on the floor around several battery-powered candles listening to a Zen Peacemakers staffer describe activities that had taken place in this block. It suddenly hit me that I might be in the exact spot where my father stood while performing his duties as a scribe. I had to lean on the person next to me for support as the domains of time and space collapsed. Looking at the ground beneath my feet, I felt an eerie closeness to that very spot.

Five straight days at Auschwitz-Birkenau left me feeling empty, too emotionally drained to distinguish between self, victim, and perpetrator. Too exhausted to blame or to hate. I came to realize the futility of any attempt to comprehend the magnitude of what had happened in this place.

As the retreat wound down, the words "Bye Bye Birkenau" came to mind, though it is doubtful that one can fully exit a realm that implants itself in your soul like a dybbuk.

The Zen Peacemakers experience shifted my focus from pondering whether I would have survived to how I could take loving action in pursuit of a more peaceful world. Having no simple formula for achieving this task, I found comfort in the words of the rabbinic sage Rabbi Tarfon: "You are not obliged to complete the work of repairing the world, but neither are you free to desist from it."

— *aron* —

Hell's Gate

It took but one hour for the train carrying Abram and several members of our family to arrive at hell's gate. Abram tells us how they were ordered to form a line and proceed slowly toward a table where a man in a white uniform decided their fate. "A slight movement of his thumb to the right or to the left," Abram writes, "was equivalent to a scythe blow from the grim reaper. That barbarian pointed my parents in the direction of the gas chambers."

It seemed out of character for Abram, a man who wrote with such emotion, to be so matter-of-fact in depicting the last time he saw his beloved mother and father alive. Perhaps it hurt too much for him to put into words what he was feeling at that moment. Whatever the reason, his compression of that climactic moment to just twelve words left me longing for more.

The man in white selected Abram, Piniek, and their youngest sister, Mania, for slave labor. Male and female prisoners were immediately relegated to different sections of the camp. Abram never saw Mania again.

Piniek's life came to a tragic end after the evacuation of Auschwitz. Abram writes:

> He and his friend Rosenzweig jumped from a moving train. Rosenzweig's head hit a hard object and began to bleed. By a true miracle, the hail of bullets the Nazi soldiers fired at them did not hit their mark. The two took refuge in a snowy forest, hoping to avoid capture. After three days in the freezing cold without food and Rosenzweig weak from the loss of blood, they gave themselves up. They were taken to a Gestapo guard post and severely beaten before being put on a train bound for the Theresienstadt concentration camp in Czechoslovakia. There they were clubbed to death along with two hundred other prisoners. Piniek died in this way only three days before Soviet troops liberated the camp.

Abram's account of Piniek's death does not square with the story I had been led to believe—that Piniek died in my father's arms on a cattle car. If Abram had known all along that Piniek was murdered in Theresienstadt, why had he insinuated that Pop was in some way responsible for Piniek's death? Abram makes no mention of what happened to Heniek, the fourth Manheimer brother, who seems to have disappeared without a trace. I have not been able to find any archival evidence of his being in Auschwitz or in any other concentration camp. All that remains is a prewar photograph of him with his girlfriend.

Return

We returned to Krakow from Birkenau on a late Friday afternoon. I spent Saturday journaling. In a stream of consciousness style, I tried to articulate what I had experienced. I wrote and wrote, stopping only for dinner with some of the other participants.

There was no place on earth I would rather have been that week. It had been the most profound experience of my life. I thought that the intensity of my Holocaust-related emotions might have eased as a result, but no.

Back in Atlanta, I was closely observed by everyone around me. They were eager to hear how the immersion affected me. I didn't have a tidy answer. Marti and the kids gave me the space to re-enter and decompress, to bear witness to my own transformation. I didn't want to talk about it. I needed to be alone. Marti thought that my somberness indicated that I might even have regressed. I assured her that I was in a good place, that healing would take time.

Past, present, and future became one. I felt an even greater love for Marti, our children, and our grandchildren as I let in the miracle of my parents' survival.

Instead of resisting poignant moments of sadness, I began to accept them, regardless of whether they diminished, increased, or remained about the same. I found myself more and more willing to give myself permission to be emotional, more willing to bear witness to myself.

— *aron* —

The Dream

After reading the translation of Abram's memoir, I had the following dream:

I am at the Auschwitz-Birkenau extermination complex. At my feet are stone steps leading down to the gas chamber. Without a hint of fear I descend and push open a steel door. I am met with a burst of radiant light. I become pure energy, at one with the universe, transcending space and time.

I awoke feeling calm but unclear about the dream's meaning. Was it a way of getting closer to the grandparents, aunts, and uncles whose earthly lives had ended in a gas chamber? Was it an unconscious wish that their deaths were not as horrific as I had always imagined, that their souls found peace in the world to come? Was it to ease my own fear of death?

Abram's memoir introduced me to lost family members I had known only by name or through a photo. He described my paternal grandfather and namesake, Aron Chaim, as a man who "wore a long beard that scissors never knew. A thick mustache covered his upper lip, and he had a broad, smooth forehead that gave him a serious and intelligent appearance. He wore a long black overcoat typical of Bedzin's Hasidic Jews. He was known as honest and pious."

Ma remembers Aron Chaim as an ascetic man who slept on a hard bench to hasten the coming of the Messiah. That is not to say that he didn't get off the bench on occasion to observe the biblical commandment to be fruitful and multiply. He fathered four sons and four daughters.

One of the most treasured possessions my parents brought to America was a tinted portrait of an old, bearded man. For my parents, having Aron Chaim's image on our living room wall was as important as affixing a *mezuzah* to our doorpost. Born in 1889, Aron Chaim Manheimer was probably in his forties when the photo was taken. We will never know the exact date of his death because the Nazis did not register names of deportees who were selected for extermination upon arrival at Auschwitz-Birkenau.

According to the *Encyclopedia of the Holocaust*, 27,000 Bedzin Jews were deported to the death camp between May 1942 and August 1943. Aron Chaim must have been fifty-three or fifty-four when he was murdered.

Abram describes his mother, Rosa, maiden name Weinrib, as a "tall woman with blue eyes and beautiful features who wore a wig in accordance with Orthodox custom. She sustained the family with the modest income she earned by running a fruit and vegetable stand in front of the apartment building where we lived."

Ma remembers Rosa as a stunningly attractive woman with blue eyes and black hair. She told me that Polish soldiers guarding the train station next door were always trying to flirt with her.

Abram describes Raquel (b. 1911), the oldest of his sisters, as having "a round face, blue eyes, thick black hair in two long braids. She excelled at school and was a source of admiration and praise. At the age of twelve, she took a job to help support the family and continued her studies at night. Her life ended in the Warsaw Ghetto along with her husband and two-year-old son, Simon." As a child, I had a particular fascination with the photo of a smiling little boy with curly locks holding a puppy. I can now attach a name to that angelic child.

Here is how Abram describes his other siblings: Tonia (b. 1913): "Tall, blue eyes, fair complexion. Her intelligence equaled that of her older sister. She married a man named Artman and they had a baby son." Tonia left the family bunker with her child to improve the chances of the others not being detected by the Nazis and was never heard from again.

Piniek (b. 1918): "Second of four sons, tall, blond, demonstrated a remarkable enterprising ability at age fifteen, when he organized a metallurgical workshop that employed dozens of workers and promised to deliver the family out of poverty." Piniek was clubbed to death by Nazis in the Theresienstadt concentration camp. After years of searching, I uncovered one sparse document referring to Piniek in the vast Holocaust archives located in Arolsen, Germany. It noted that Pinkus Mannheimer was born February 11, 1918, and died April 17, 1945. This rare fragment is as meaningful to me as a gravestone.

Pola (b. 1920): "Cheerful, petite, dark hair, beautiful singing voice." She was captured during a Nazi raid of her house in Bedzin and died in Auschwitz-Birkenau with her husband.

Mania (b. 1921): "A singular beauty, tall, blonde, blue eyes, graceful, radiating kindness." Unsure of her fate, Abram writes, "She lasts in the memory of those who knew and loved her."

Morris Rosen knew and loved Mania. He was from Ma's town of Dabrowa. I met him at the 1995 gathering of death march survivors in the Czech Republic town of Volary. He told me: "Mania was my girlfriend in a forced labor camp of thirty prisoners. Mania was the only woman and did the cooking. Her beauty aroused a lot of jealousy. One day one of the laborers reported to the Nazis that she was giving larger portions to her brother, Piniek, and she was expelled. Mania died of TB in another camp."

Heniek (b. 1922): "Tall, athletic, dark hair, blue eyes, popular with the girls." His fate is unknown.

That is all I know about Pop's murdered family members. There are no tombstones inscribed with their names. I hold them in inherited memory and in dreams.

A Book?

Shortly after my return from the Zen Peacekeepers retreat, I shared some of my experiences on Facebook. A friend responded, "I smell a book here!" I thought it was a good idea but wasn't prepared to take it on. After six months, I mentioned to Aron that I was seriously considering writing a book about what it was like growing up as a child of survivors and how it has impacted my life.

Aron's response surprised me. "Why don't we write a joint memoir?" I knew instantly that this was the way to go. What better partner for this project? Aron had been a professional editor for fifty years and my friend even longer. Two days later, I booked a flight to Connecticut.

— *aron* —

Let's Do It

In the spring of 2019, Marty brought up the idea of writing a book about growing up as a son of Holocaust survivors. I said, "Let's do it together." The idea appealed to me as a transitional project in advance of my impending retirement from the Union for Reform Judaism. Marty was thrilled with the idea.

We initially conceived of the book as a freewheeling dialogue, along the lines of *The Dude and the Zenmaster*, in which Jeff Bridges and Bernie Glassman exchanged views on how to do good in the world. In June, Marty came to Connecticut for several days to begin recording a series of conversations. It soon became clear that there were huge gaps in what we each knew about our families' Holocaust histories. It felt like the right time to find out what we could.

— *marty* —

Cracks in the Darkness

Aron and I began sharing the bits of information we were able to dig up. Some were so horrific that they cannot be blotted out, ever.

Before sharing Abram's account of how the Nazis broke through the bunker and prepared to send the last Jews of Bedzin to Auschwitz, Aron phoned to give me a heads up that I should prepare myself before reading it. All he would say was that my father's two young daughters, who were also caught while in hiding, might have shared the same fate.

Feeling my throat tighten up, I thought this sounded like one of the terrible truths my parents had tried to shield me from. I began planning when to read Aron's piece. I figured I'd wait a couple of days but decided it would be better to get it over with and braced myself.

I couldn't help but relate to the people in the story, as if what had happened to them had happened to me. I surprised myself by holding it together emotionally while reading the piece. That lasted until Abram's haunting description of how the Nazis disposed of the children. Lusha and Ruthie could well have been among them. I'll never know if my father witnessed this terrible scene, or one similar.

I once asked my father if he had ever gotten drunk. He said, "Only one time. The night before the liquidation of the ghetto."

The image of little children being thrown into sacks like animals bound for the slaughter is indelibly etched in my mind. I do not regret that, for I believe that light shines through the cracks in the darkness when we refuse to blot out what is most painful to us and bear witness.

— *aron* —

The Price of Revenge

I had known since childhood that Pop was shot through the chest by an SS guard after jumping from a moving train, but I had few details about the chronology of events. I knew from Pop's Auschwitz ID card that he arrived in October 1942 and was evacuated on January 25, 1945, only four days before Soviet troops liberated the surviving prisoners.

As a participant in a 2009 Jewish press tour of the International Red Cross Archives in Arolsen, Germany, I was handed a document listing February 16, 1945, as the day Pop arrived at Gusen II, a subcamp of Mauthausen. I could hardly believe that only three weeks after being shot, Pop was a prisoner once again in another notorious concentration camp. Even worse, having been branded an escapee, he was subjected to "special punishment," administered by a sadistic Roma kapo who would cane him at every opportunity.

Soldiers of the United States 11th Armored Division liberated Mauthausen on May 5, 1945. They found Pop alive, his emaciated body among a stack of corpses.

I was aware that Pop had exacted revenge on the kapo who tormented him in Mauthausen. Beyond that, I knew little else about what had transpired.

I asked my sister what she knew about the kapo incident and was surprised to learn that she had talked to Pop about it in some detail. When Rose was in her mid-twenties, she decided to write a piece about our parents' Holocaust experiences to get a better sense of how they impacted her own life. She sat down with Pop one afternoon and asked him to tell her exactly what happened to him in the immediate aftermath of his liberation from Mauthausen.

According to Rose's notes, Pop went for a walk in a nearby village with his friend Moniek. Pop stopped in front of a shop and looked at his reflection in the window. Peering back at him was this strange fellow with a crazed look, his body little more than bones. He asked Moniek, "Who's this man staring at me?" Moniek said, "Wolf, that's you."

Pop described how he felt at that moment: "I looked again and could see nothing familiar about this man. How is it possible for a human being to change so much? I was such a strong man. I sat down on the curb and wept like a baby. I had nothing in the world, no family, not even myself."

His lament was interrupted by the sound of a man singing in German. Pop turned around and saw the kapo who had tormented him in Mauthausen approaching.

"When our eyes met," Pop recalled, "the kapo yelled, 'Oh! It's you, the dirty Jew. Why didn't I finish you off when I had the chance?' My blood boiled. Moniek and I forced him into an alley and with all my strength I plunged a knife into his stomach, payback for all the suffering and death inflicted on my family, for stealing my youth, my health, my future."

Pop and Moniek fled the scene and joined a passing column of repatriated French slave laborers. The two fugitives marched with them to an airport. During the pre-boarding roll call, Pop and Moniek responded, "*Oui*" and replaced two absent Frenchmen on the flight. In Paris, Pop was cut off from the humanitarian aid distributed to displaced persons in occupied Germany.

Ma filled me in on what happened next: "In Paris, Pop had little to eat and lived mostly on wine. Already weak from years of deprivation, his health quickly deteriorated. Abram was searching for him everywhere. Then one day he got word from another Bedzin survivor, Sala Leitner, that Wolf was a patient in the Rothschild Hospital in Paris. Abram found Pop asleep. He waited. When Pop opened his eyes and saw his youngest brother, he was too overwhelmed to speak. For a long time, they just looked at one another in silence."

Abram writes, "When I found Wolf, he could not explain how he was still alive. The mistreatment, the punishments, the forced labor, the poor diet had taken their toll. His body was swollen like a balloon. The slightest movement caused him intense pain. His body resembled a rag doll made up of different pieces about to come apart."

Abram managed to smuggle Pop out of France. "Without documents or money," he writes, "we used cunning and luck. On the train to Germany, we intermingled with a large contingent of Polish officers. Conversing and drinking vodka, we managed to avoid the conductor for the twenty-four-hour journey. We were met in Feldafing by my wife and his girlfriend, whom I had previously met." The "girlfriend," of course, was Ma.

Pop was admitted to a sanitorium in the town of Gauting, a short distance from Feldafing. It was housed in what had been a luxurious castle called Schloss Elmau in the Bavarian Alps. The American occupation forces had requisitioned the property and converted it into a tuberculosis sanatorium for Holocaust survivors.

From there, Pop was transferred to a hospital in Heidelberg to undergo thoracoplasty, a surgical technique requiring the resection of multiple ribs to collapse the lung in the hope of inactivating the disease. Sedated only with schnapps, Wolf watched the operation in a mirror. He was given too much oxygen, which tore a hole in one of his lungs. Pop lived the rest of his life with only partial lung function. I'll never know if Pop regretted the act of vengeance that would cost him his health.

Years ago, I wrote an article titled "Knowledge Makes You Free." After reading Abram's memoir, I stopped believing that learning facts, like how our family members were savaged and murdered, could bring me peace of mind. On the contrary, every new revelation has been agonizing.

One evening at our weekly family Shabbat dinner, I looked across the table and took delight in the sparkle in our grandchildren's eyes as Judy lit the candles. I was suddenly struck with the terrible thought that one and a half million children *just like them* were slaughtered in Europe for no reason other than having been born Jewish. I kept this fleeting thought to myself and moved on, trying to enjoy the rest of the evening.

Moments of joy sometimes trigger feelings of great sorrow in me. These two seemingly contradictory emotions live side by side. Jewish tradition does not encourage us to untangle gladness from sadness. Even on the happiest of occasions, such as a Jewish wedding, we are commanded to remember the destruction of the Holy Temple in Jerusalem. To maintain my equilibrium, I strive to balance what haunts me with love and with hope.

Too Much

While Aron felt compelled to continue researching his family's past, I questioned my desire to know more about mine. Delving into my past has not become any easier. My participation with the Zen Peacemakers notwithstanding, I continue to feel a strong impulse to resist learning "too much."

Though writing this memoir has required that I deepen my inquiry into subjects I had previously avoided, my first reaction to new information is to put off looking at it. When Aron sent me a link to a new ninety-minute documentary about the liquidation of the ghetto in Sosnowiec, the town where my mother lived, I had to force myself to watch it.

The film gave a chronological account of what happened from the initial German occupation of Sosnowiec until the liquidation of the Jewish population in August 1943. Once into it, I found myself genuinely interested in learning details of how the story unfolded. I studied each photo, hoping to identify a familiar face, maybe my mother's. I held it together emotionally until the very end, at which point I allowed myself a short, cathartic cry. Of particular significance is that I watched the film to the end, undeterred by the iron gate that had previously kept me from getting too close. As I continue to muster the courage to "go deeper," I am less fearful that I will lose myself in an abyss of sadness and despair.

I sometimes regret not having asked my parents about their lives before the war, how they survived, how they found the courage to reconstruct their lives after the war. Yet, I instinctively avoided going down that terrible tunnel. I didn't want to know more than I could handle. Aron shared a poem written by his Uncle Abram. In it, he asks, "*Vi haltmen dos ois?*" How can we endure this? Perhaps the answer is best expressed in the central image of Edvard Munch's painting, "The Scream."

I would have wanted my father to know that even absent the details, I "got him" and that I saw my life as his victory over the Nazis. I've always believed that he knew this, but my acknowledgement might have eased the burden of his loss and brought him a measure of comfort.

— *aron* —

Volary Revisited

The trip to Volary had been a life affirming event for Ma and illuminating for Rose and me. We had learned much about the fate of the victims, but what of their tormentors? Had they been brought to justice?

After the war, survivors of the death march identified Hungarian German Michael Weingaertner as the man who shot twenty-two women near Volary. His pregnant girlfriend, Ruth Schultz, was the guard sitting next to Ma who was hit when the truck came under fire by the American fighter plane. A few days later, Weingaertner and two other male guards escaped by foot over the border into Austria. The chief woman guard, Herta Breitman, was also wounded in the aerial attack. She received medical treatment in the Volary hospital and later escaped from an American internment camp.

Only two of the death march guards were held accountable for their war crimes. Ruth Hildner was found guilty in a Czech court and hanged on May 2, 1947. Commander Alois Dorr was found guilty of murder in a German court in 1969 and sentenced to life in prison. He was released after serving ten years and died of natural causes in 1990.

Daniel Goldhagen's book, *Hitler's Willing Executioners*, reveals that only one of the death march guards was a card-carrying Nazi. The others were *not* SS members, as Ma always thought. They were volunteers who had nothing better to do. The men signed on because they were unsuitable for military service. The women were bored in their menial jobs and wanted some fun, to meet men, to have adventures.

As edifying as the Volary reunion was for me, discovering that ordinary Germans were capable of such horrific crimes against innocent Jewish women left me shaken, angry, and dispirited. Goldhagen's revelation, more than any other, upended my belief that knowledge makes you free.

— *marty* —

Photos in a Drawer

The framed portrait of my father's first family has hung in our downstairs hallway for almost forty years. Before the Zen Peacemakers immersion, I paid it little attention because it evoked such feelings of sorrow. Today I regard it as a kind of mini-sanctuary, like a Buddhist memorial shrine. I take notice of Lusha smiling at the camera with that "Yura twinkle" in her eyes and how her younger sister, Ruthie, looks so serious. Dad and Gutcha project "photograph smiles," almost forced. At times I wonder if they had any inkling of what was about to befall them.

This image was likely hidden somewhere in Bedzin and retrieved after the war. At some point, a large pencil rendering of the original photo was made by someone who depicted my father with a mustache, though he was fully shaven in the photo. I assume that the artist must have known that Dad had sported a mustache before the war. I saw the drawing for the first time after Mom and I returned to Los Angeles from Israel in 1975. It was rolled up and stored in a closet. I didn't look at the drawing again until 1984, when Marti and I went to Los Angeles for a visit and my mother gave it to me. Marti insisted that we have it framed and displayed in our home.

I didn't expect any more pre-war photos of my family to turn up. Two years ago, Cousin Rita phoned me to inquire if I knew who might have left her an envelope containing a small cache of family photographs that she uncovered in a drawer not opened in years. I knew nothing of their existence. How any of these images had survived and made their way into our hands remains a mystery.

The black and white snapshots depict Bedzin Jews enjoying the moment, oblivious to the unimaginable catastrophe about to destroy their world. I was shocked to see my father with Gutcha, whom I "knew" only from the portrait. One photo captures them standing together in front of a tree, staring adoringly at one another. Another shows them gently touching while seated among a group of friends. I had never even imagined my father enjoying his life in Poland before the Nazi invasion, nor having been close and intimate with Gutcha. It struck me that, had Gutcha survived, I would not exist.

These long-forgotten photos introduced a new twist in my perception of my father's life. I began to picture him relating to his girls, my sisters, with the love and affection he had always shown me. I've often thought how much delight he would have taken in meeting my kids and grandkids.

I find comfort in knowing that my father had experienced a time of happiness and contentment before the war. Perhaps that is the message that the person who saved these photos wished to convey.

— *aron* —

Ma Marches On

Having learned as much as I could from Abram's memoir and other historical sources about the Manheimers of Bedzin, I turned my attention to Ma's side of the family.

Even at her advanced age, Ma is a reliable source of information. She is now 105 years old and, as she puts it, "I still have my marbles." What could she tell me about her father, Hemia? "He was a *tzaddik*, a righteous man. What mattered most to him was *tzedakah*, acts of charity, and I think it is because he was orphaned at the age of five." Ma remembers her mother, Eleanor, as a "humble woman who doted on her only child. When I wanted to help her in the kitchen, she would say, 'You have time to learn how to cook. Go read a book instead.'" To this day, Ma doesn't know how to bake a cake.

When I asked her what were the most important lessons she learned from her parents, she said, "My father taught me that love comes to you when you give it to others, and what matters most in life is to have a good name because that is all that remains after you're gone."

"When the Nazis entered Dabrowa and burned down the synagogue, Ma's mother said to her, "I see that we are going to be separated soon. Remember one thing: If somebody hits you, don't hit back because two bads don't make a good. You will be rewarded, but you have to be patient."

Eleanor died in Auschwitz at the age of fifty-three. Ma remembers the last time she saw her mother alive: "I was with a group of girls in Sosnowiec about to be transported to a concentration camp. From a distance I saw my mother coming toward me. She was holding a piece of cheesecake. A Nazi guard beat her to the ground. There was nothing I could do to help her."

When I asked Ma if she is ever able to put that terrible past behind her, she said, "I can never block the Holocaust from my mind. Every time I sit down to eat, I think of how terribly hungry I was in the concentration camp and on the death march. What they fed us was barely enough to keep us alive. A morsel of potato, beet, or cabbage would be like a gourmet meal." In our home, wasting food was a *shanda*, a sin. Rose remembers how sharply Ma scolded her for the sin of pouring a glass of carrot-veggie juice in the toilet. Ma too has never forgotten that episode.

These days, when we visit Ma and sit down for a meal, she insists on serving herself. "In my house," she says, "I choose what to eat, not like it was in the concentration camp."

Ma believes that a higher power "is leading my life." To prove her point, she recently told me the following story: "Every Sunday in Grünberg, the Nazis would make us line up and count off. If you came up number ten, you were sent to Auschwitz. My number was always nine or eleven. That had to be more than just luck." She had many other close calls during her years in Nazi captivity, but the one she remembers most vividly occurred during the death march.

> I noticed a doghouse in a nearby yard and left the line hoping to find some food scraps. My action was observed by a fearsome

guard known as "Der Sheeser," the shooter. We gave him that name because he took pleasure in shooting girls in the head with his little golden pistol. Seeing him approach me, I knew my life was about to end. I dropped my most valuable possession—a little pillow—and began reciting the Shema. At that moment a miracle happened. Instead of shooting me, Der Sheeser yelled at me for daring to walk away in broad daylight. He ordered me to get back in the line and to keep marching. Along the road, he handed me my pillow.

"Whatever happens to me," Ma often says, "was meant to be. I don't know who is pulling the strings, but something is watching over me. Maybe it's because my father was such a *tzaddik*, righteous man. No matter how bad things got, I never lost hope. If I didn't live with hope, I wouldn't be here. You and Rose wouldn't be here."

— *marty* —
Light at the End of the Tunnel

For as long as I can remember, the Holocaust has been the dominant and defining context of my life. That it could even have happened haunts me, as does the question: How could God, if there is a God, have allowed it to happen? For most of my life I've managed to keep a cautious distance from this upsetting, even despairing, question. During my youth, I just didn't talk about the Holocaust. During my military service, I fought on the side dedicated to preventing it from happening again. While raising my family, I tried to push it away, to avoid crossing the line and succumbing to an unstoppable surge of sadness and tears.

I can now experience this loss, this sadness, and not be carried away by it. I've reached a point where the past informs but does not dictate my life.

— *aron* —

Fear of Crying

For fifty years as a journalist and author, I took every opportunity to learn as much as possible about the Holocaust. In researching my family history for this memoir, I exhausted every available resource, peered under every rock. Yet there is so much more that I don't know and never will. Surely new information, fresh clues will come to light. But continuing my search feels like fighting an unceasing tide, constantly ebbing and flowing, pulling me back, then thrusting me farther away.

I have always found it hard to cry, afraid to let my emotions distract me from the needs of the moment, and not crying was a way to shield myself from the emotional aftershocks reverberating through the survivor ecosystem. I feared that even a single teardrop could unleash an endless torrent.

During my visit to Buenos Aires to attend Raquel and Jose's wedding, Abram recited his Yiddish poem *"Vi Haltmen Dus Oise?"* (How Can One Endure This?), questioning how prisoners were able to withstand the torturous conditions of the camps and death marches.

Hearing his heartbreaking lament, I didn't shed a tear. Raquel was incredulous. "How can you be so unfeeling?" In my defense, I insisted that each of us expresses emotion in our own way. Raquel's words came to mind fifteen years later, when I did not cry upon receiving news of Pop's death or while delivering a eulogy at his funeral.

Last year on Yom Kippur, after lighting a *yahrzeit* candle to honor my father's memory, I sat down and read out loud the text of that eulogy for the first time in forty years.

> My father was a quiet man. He was not one to engage in philosophical or political discussions. He did not tell people what to think or how to live. Pop was a man of few words. He did not have answers to life's haunting questions. To his dying day, he did not know why he was chosen to suffer. "Why?" he would ask, "When I wanted to live, they would not let me and when I wanted to die, they would not let me." *Ma lot nisht lebn, Ma lot nisht shtarben.*

The doctors never fully understood my father's intense will to survive. They called him "Miracle Man," but did not think his life was worth the effort to save him. They called in my mother and informed her of their opinion. She said, "Never will I allow you to finish Hitler's work."

So moved were the doctors that they gave her a crash course in respiratory therapy and sent my father home in her care. She converted their bedroom into a veritable intensive care unit and nursed him body and soul almost twenty-four hours a day for the next five years. She is a "miracle woman."

I read the eulogy and cried.

— *marty* —

A Mushy Man

When I was a kid, adults in my family didn't cry. The only exception I can recall was when my mother received the news of President John F. Kennedy's assassination.

I don't know if my parents had learned to suppress their emotions as a way to be strong during the war and its aftermath. Perhaps they had already shed a lifetime of tears. I do know that their softness and compassion was not compromised; they were always loving and kind. Perhaps they just wanted to conceal their past trauma from "*de kind*," the kid, as they referred to me.

If my elders were trying to model some kind of stoicism for my benefit, it didn't work. When I was about seven years old, Mom and I were in our living room listening to the radio when a story came on about a child with polio. I became overwhelmed with sadness and began to cry, something I didn't do readily in her presence. What affected me most was the heartbreak and sorrow of the child's parents. Mom held and hugged me, but I couldn't be consoled.

I've come to fully accept myself as a mushy man. With age I've gotten even mushier. I no longer consider my tendency to cry easily a cause for shame or embarrassment. I've learned not to resist it but instead to allow my cathartic bursts to pass within seconds, relieving the buildup of raw emotion.

Recently, I had a breakthrough. I heard a voice inside shout, *Geneeg!* (Enough!)

Enough of this victimization. Enough of living with the fear of imminent calamity. Enough of being a powerless pawn in my own life story. I have discovered an EXIT door next to the familiar door leading to a tunnel of turbulence and upset.

My ability to experience intense emotions is still part of who I am. What has changed is my ability to choose which door to enter whenever my emotions are triggered by threats, real or imagined.

There's some solace in all this. I am grateful for having a high degree of empathy and compassion. I am grateful to those closest to me for understanding and allowing me to express my emotions freely.

Perhaps part of my legacy is that I have the capacity to tap into the reservoir of tears that the survivors in my family declared off limits.

— *aron* —

The Power of Love

The trauma I inherited from my parents is as much a part of my genetic makeup as the color of my eyes, and it manifests itself most palpably when I spend a few days in the presence of my mother.

It wasn't until Judy and I stayed at Ma's house in Los Angeles for a week to celebrate her 103rd birthday that I became fully aware of the emotions these visits stir up in me. Hugging Ma when she greets us at the door always fills me with joy. After a day or two, a feeling of unease begins to well up inside me. Ma invariably pulls out photos of me as a little boy, transporting me to a time when I felt helpless in coping with my parents' sorrow and loss. Ma tells me that as a young child I would bang my head on the wall for no apparent reason.

I respect and admire Ma for her courage, perseverance, and loving spirit. But when we are together, the line between first- and second-generation blurs. I feel myself regressing to the time before my visit to Bedzin, before the invisible number vanished from my arm.

Though Pop was a stay-at-home dad, Ma had the greatest influence on me. She imbued me with the notion that saving for a rainy day is a good survival strategy. In concentration camp, she found it more advantageous to nibble on a concealed potato for a few days than to gulp it down. Better to have something than nothing. During the death march, she traded a piece of raw beet for a dab of ointment to treat an infected boil on her neck, which saved her life.

After the liberation, Ma saw some survivors in the DP camp eating cheese, a pricey source of protein. She located the vendor but couldn't bring herself to splurge on this luxury. Instead, she bought a couple of apples to share with Pop. The next day, the local currency crashed. Ma tossed her worthless money into a garbage pail. She regretted not buying the cheese, but by then self-denial and living on little had become a fixed habit, a way of life.

Ma once told me how much she regrets having missed out on vacations and other good times because of Pop's infirmities. I advised, "It's never too late to change your ways. The rabbis taught that self-deprivation is as sinful as overindulgence." She replied, "I want to love myself more, but at my age, I can't change."

What keeps Ma going is her love of family and belief in humanity. Every night before she goes to sleep, Ma recites this prayer: "*A gitte nakht mine kinde, mine einiklekh, mine ei-einiklakh, und alle gitte menschen oft de velt*" (A good night my children, grandchildren, great-grandchildren, and all the good people of the world).

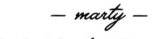

Not Just Another Yom Kippur

Marti and our kids would always give me a wide berth on Yom Kippur. On the holiest day of the Jewish year, the time for atonement and judgment, I would almost automatically retreat into an inner world, awash with images of death and suffering. Appreciation and gratitude for my blessings of health, family, and loving relationships were put on temporary hold. It was as if Yom Kippur provided an excuse to "backslide" into an abyss, reinforcing my belief that to be a Jew is to suffer. Making matters worse, I associated the holiday with the pain and death I witnessed at close range on the battlefield of the Yom Kippur War.

Before Aron and I embarked on this book project in 2018 I had essentially written off observance of Yom Kippur, going about business as usual. After two years of collaboration with Aron, I decided to observe the holiday in my own way, though I did not know in what way.

I arranged for a substitute to teach my Monday morning yoga class and used the time to meditate and do some easy yoga. I decided to make it a day of fasting, a traditional Jewish practice on Yom Kippur that I had not followed for several years. Later in the day I did another meditation on my screened porch followed by savasana, a supine, closed-eyes, half-asleep yoga pose.

I then took a long, leisurely walk, enjoying the fall foliage as I listened to an audio book by Pema Chodron on Buddhist meditation. The theme was "*maitri*," the Sanskrit word for loving kindness, which she describes as "complete acceptance of ourselves as we are" and "unconditional friendliness."

Unlike in past years, when I would withdraw into myself on Yom Kippur, this time I was present, calm, engaged with how the day was unfolding before me. I was able to let go of the predictable narrative and behaviors to which I had become habituated over so many years. I experienced a newfound freedom, grounded in a feeling of loving kindness toward myself—a transformation!

Aron phoned shortly after I returned home from my walk. He asked if he could read me the eulogy he had delivered at his father's funeral and hadn't looked at again until today. Aron was all choked up as he shared with me how his father's last wish was that he light a *yahrzeit* candle on the anniversary of his death. Then I told Aron how my dad had always introduced me to his friends as his *kaddish*—the son who would recite the mourners' prayer for him each year on the anniversary of his passing. Here we were, sons of Holocaust survivors tenderly remembering our fathers on the day Jews traditionally recite a prayer in memory of loved ones.

This intensely emotional exchange, I realized, had not pushed me back into the familiar dark hole of sadness and depression that I usually experienced on Yom Kippur. Nor had it undone the ease and calm I had experienced earlier in the day.

For the first time as an adult I could just "be" on Yom Kippur, informed by the past but not hostage to it. The following Yom Kippur I went even further, fasting for twenty-four hours and live streaming worship services from the Park Avenue Synagogue in New York. I actually enjoyed the experience, remembering many of the prayers and melodies from my youth. I felt at home, inspired, engaged. Gone were my Yom Kippur demons of the past.

— *aron* —

October 7, 2023

Abram wrote his poem *"Vi Haltmen Dos Ois?"* (How Do We Endure This?") in the context of the Holocaust, but it is a question that Jews have asked in perilous times ever since our ancestors first stepped onto the stage of history. Every great catastrophe that has befallen the Jewish people is commemorated in our holiday cycle. On the fast day of *Tisha B'av* (the ninth of the Jewish month of *Av*), the saddest day in the Jewish calendar, we mourn the destruction of the ancient Temples in Jerusalem, the expulsions of the Jews from England and Spain, the massacres of medieval Jewish communities by the Crusaders. Every year on *Yom Hashoah* we light candles in solemn remembrance of the Six Million. The Hamas pogrom of October 7, 2023, resulting in the murder of more than 1,200 Israeli men, women, and children, is the latest in this chain of catastrophes.

The day after the Hamas attack, Ma phoned me in tears. "Will Israel survive?" "Of course," I assured her, though I was re-experiencing the sense of the dread I felt as a UCLA sophomore at the start of the June 1967 Arab-Israeli war. I texted Adi Aronow, a dear friend in Israel: How are you? She replied: "It's the worst war we have ever known. My neighbor's friend was just murdered in front of his kids." I posed the same question to Michael Gordon, my best friend from Cleveland who lives in Jerusalem. "Personally we're fine," he texted back, "but yesterday will probably go down as the most tragic single day in the history of the State of Israel. One heart-rending story after another."

Hearing news reports of Hamas terrorists decapitating Jewish babies, burning people alive, raping and butchering women, and carting away captives brought to mind Abram's description of Nazis stuffing crying Jewish children into sacks and hauling them off to their deaths in Auschwitz. Not since Hitler have the Jewish people faced an enemy as dedicated to the mass murder of Jews as Hamas.

At the time of this writing, the Israeli-Hamas war has been raging for many months. The loss of so many innocent lives in Gaza is also excruciating for me to bear. It is a great tragedy that will traumatize Palestinians for generations to come, just as October 7 and its aftermath will leave lasting scars on the Israeli psyche. The Talmud teaches: "To save one life is to save the world" (Sanhedrin 37a). Nothing would be more tragic than to allow the actions of our enemies to cause us to become indifferent to the suffering of innocent people. My own humanity demands no less.

Ma now ends every phone call with the Jewish rallying cry *"Am Yisrael Chai!"* (The Jewish People Live!) Though Ma is one of the few remaining Holocaust survivors in Los Angeles, she did not attend the 2024 community-wide *Yom HaShoah* commemoration because she feared a terrorist attack. She has stopped going to Club Europa, the weekly gathering of survivors. When I asked her why, she said, "Until the war ends, I cannot be in a place where people dance."

Equanimity Upended

To describe my reaction to the October 7 Hamas attack as déjà vu would be a gross understatement. It came only a day after the fiftieth anniversary of the 1973 Yom Kippur War, when I went to war as an officer in the

Israel Defense Forces on the Golan Heights. In the years that followed, I became much more accepting of myself for what I considered sins of commission as well as sins of omission as a soldier. My attention always seemed to be drawn toward the cost of victories: friends and comrades fallen and injured. A half century since my naivete about war was shattered, I felt more grounded and clear, far more able to resist getting "hooked" than before. The Hamas assault upended my sense of equanimity.

When asked by friends and acquaintances how I was doing in the aftermath of the Hamas attack on October 7, I said, "Okay." I avoided disclosing how not okay I was, realizing how much more okay I was than almost anyone living in Israel or in Gaza. Like any compassionate human being, I was deeply affected by the sheer shock of the brutality perpetrated by Hamas on so many Jews and the loss and suffering of so many Palestinians in the line of Israeli fire.

— *aron* —

The Surviving Remnant

For a brief period after their liberation in 1945, many survivors adopted the slogan "Never Again!" They believed that their testimony would prevent such horrors from ever recurring. They were wrong. Speaking at the closing ceremony of the first World Gathering of Jewish Holocaust survivors in Jerusalem on June 18, 1981, Elie Wiesel expressed their disillusionment:

> We must ask ourselves painful questions: Have we survivors done our duty? Has our warning been properly articulated? Has our message? Have we acted as true witnesses? It is with fear and trembling that we often reach the conclusion that something went wrong with our testimony; otherwise things would have been different. Look at the world around us: violence everywhere, hatred everywhere, state-sponsored terror, racism, fascism, fanaticism, antisemitism. Had anyone told us when we were liberated that we would be compelled in our lifetime to fight antisemitism once

more, or worse, that we would have to prove that our suffering was genuine, that our victims had indeed perished, we would have had no strength to lift up our eyes from the ruins. . . .

And yet, we shall not give up, we shall not give in. It may be too late for the victims and even for the survivors—but not for our children, not for mankind. In a society of bigotry and indifference, we must tell our contemporaries that whatever the answer, it must grow out of human compassion and reflect man's relentless quest for justice and memory.

The corollary to the question, How we can bear so much suffering? is Why don't we just give up? Many Jews have done just that. Throughout history, whenever the gates of assimilation opened, the majority of Jews took the nearest exit. Marty and I are among the determined minority who will never give up, never give in. We have followed in our parents' footsteps, identifying with the *She'erit ha-Pleita*, the surviving remnant, the term liberated Jews in the DP camps adopted to define themselves. Marty and I cannot be anything but Jewish. We own our otherness.

We are Jews by choice, endowed by our ancestors with a sacred mission. The ancient rabbis asserted that the central task of Jews, the very purpose of our lives, is to play a transcendent role in the redemption of our world. According to the great kabbalist Isaac Luria (1534–1572), when God created the world, some of the divine light became trapped in husks. The function of humans is to find and break open these husks in order to release the hidden light. In this radical reinterpretation of the Talmudic concept of *tikkun olam*, the healing of one's own soul shifted to the healing of the world. Thus did the redemption of the world become a Jewish imperative, our reason for being.

As Rabbi Hertzberg and I wrote in *Jews: The Essence and Character of a People*, "To be a Jew is to be commanded, to take actions because they are right, not because they bring personal comfort or gain. To be a Jew is to believe that the world can be redeemed. To be a Jew is to be carried by the current of an ancient Jewish river that keeps on flowing."

epilogue

A Legacy of Love Against Hate

— *aron* —

I did not try to conceal the Holocaust from our children. They knew from a young age that Hitler and the Nazis had done terrible things to my parents and other family members.

Mimi was only six years old when she engaged me in the following conversation:

"What happens if I fall in love and want to marry someone who is not Jewish?"

"If you are in love, that would be okay."

"What happens if I fall in love and want to marry someone who is German?"

"If you're in love, that would be okay."

"What if I fall in love with a Nazi and I want to marry him?"

"That would not be okay. You can't marry a Nazi."

"What if he's a good Nazi?"

"There are no good Nazis."

At Ridgefield High School, Mimi chose German to satisfy her language requirement.

"Why German?" I asked.

"I wanted to learn Yiddish in order to feel more connected to Grandma Adela, but Yiddish was not offered."

"Don't you think it was ironic to choose German as a way of feeling closer to a Holocaust survivor?"

"No. Every interaction I've had with a German person has been really lovely. So I don't see that connection between Germans and Nazis now, even though I obviously was working through it as a child."

Mimi participated in a Ridgefield-Überlingen student exchange program. Our visiting student, Verena, arrived on a Friday night. It was also the anniversary of Pop's death. As I looked at the *yahrzeit* candle we had lit in his memory, my mind flashed back to the time I traveled with him to Israel. As it happened, our itinerary included an overnight stopover in Frankfurt, Germany. Just hearing airport guards conversing in German was enough to unnerve me. In disgust, I turned to Pop and said, "Those damn Germans!" His response surprised me: "Not all Germans were bad." Pop's words came to mind on that first Shabbat with Verena.

The following summer Mimi stayed with Verena's family in Überlingen, a town on the shore of Lake Constance near the border with Switzerland. Her father sent us a letter asking permission for Mimi to join his family on a visit to a concentration camp memorial site. We had no objection. After a long car ride, they arrived at Dachau. Mimi knew exactly what to do. She placed a stone on the monument and recited Kaddish. I asked her recently what that experience was like for her. She said, "I felt a strong connection to my people. I also felt a powerful sense of defiance. My existence proved that we could not be eliminated."

Years later Mimi visited Verena in Munich, only sixteen miles from my birthplace, Feldafing. She was surprised that the former displaced persons camp was situated in a very affluent Bavarian town on the shore of scenic Lake Starnberg. Hearing this, I wondered if my parents had taken in the picturesque landscape visible through the barbed-wire fence encircling the camp. They must have at least had a sense of place, or why else would they have outfitted their three-year-old in lederhosen and a little green Tyrolean hat for our voyage to America?

Mimi identifies more with my generation than with hers. "I don't feel that the Holocaust happened way in the past," she says. "I feel like it's very close, like it happened to us, to our immediate family." Mimi believes that the status quo is temporary and that something dark lurks around the corner that could come for us at any time. "I never feel totally safe," she says. "I fear it could happen to us again in my lifetime, and we must be ready. The idea that everything can be gone in a minute and that you need an escape plan is very essential to who I am. I learned that from you."

Our son Isaac has expressed similar fears. "The Jewish people must never be complacent, he says, "because our enemies are always waiting for an opportunity to bring us down." After completing a program in permaculture design at Kibbutz Lotan in Israel, Isaac built his own ecovillage in Ghana, West Africa, partly as a bridge between cultures and partly as a family refuge. "It is a good practice, he says, "not to have all our eggs in one basket. With so much upheaval in the world, having branches of our family in Argentina, Canada, the US, and Africa makes a lot of sense."

Our son Noah, who joined me on a trip to Auschwitz-Birkenau when he was in his early twenties, recognizes that Jews are a vulnerable people, but says he doesn't feel any residual trauma. "I don't look at the Holocaust as something that happened to me in the sense that I carry a wound that needs to heal," he says. "I see our family's survival as more of a story of victory than of victimization." Noah believes that our family is blessed and that it is our destiny to ultimately survive any threat or hardship. He has felt the presence of a guardian angel throughout his life, especially at those times when he was in real danger, like when a fellow student went on a deadly shooting spree during Noah's freshman year at Simon's Rock College.

Mimi, Isaac, Noah, and their spouses have continued the family tradition of telling their children about the Holocaust. Nothing has been more impactful on our seven grandchildren than being with their centenarian great-grandmother, whom they regard with awe and reverence.

At the age of nine, Skylar, the younger daughter of Noah and Susi, wrote a story for a public-school assignment in which she imagined herself as my mother, Adela, during the Holocaust. Her writing was uncannily faithful to the experience of our family in Poland, from hiding and deportation to escape and liberation. Skylar's story begins:

> There was snow on the ground, and it was dead silent in town. I was cramped in a bunker with my family, hungry and cold. All my close friends were killed or taken to concentration camps. I was looking around and saw what felt like a prison. My parents were praying, and I was sitting on the ground silently. I had a thin blanket on, but that didn't help. I was still shivering and cold. "Adela, are you OK?" my mom said. "Yes, I'm just cold." "OK," said my worried mom. She whispered something to my dad. I overheard her say, "She is only 16."

The story ends with the Nazis forcing Adela and her friend Julie to line up before a firing squad.

> WAKE UP! MOVE IT.... His voice was rough, and I could not understand him that well because of his accent. I did as I was told and got in the line next to Julie. I can't let her die, not like this. We were in the second row. The Nazis got a third row of people to go in the line, but at that moment I grabbed Julie's hand not knowing if I was doing the right thing. We ran as fast as we could to the shed that was next to us. "Adela," she whispered, "what are you doing?" "Saving your life," I said. Now we have a long journey to get home. I shivered as I looked out to the distance. I was leaving behind my family and everything I loved and was thinking that I had nothing left to count on.

Amazed at how well Skylar had internalized Ma's story of survival, I asked her why she chose to write about this topic. She replied, "I was curious about how Grandma Adela made it through the death march."

— *marty* —

I made no attempt to conceal my parents' tragic legacy from my three children. I simply avoided the subject, which only made them more inquisitive about where I was coming from as a parent.

Andrea, whom I had adopted when I married Marti, observed that my life's mission has been to figure out whether a given situation is safe or not. She says that I have passed down that mindset to her. Andrea thoroughly researches every product, like a car seat for her son, to be sure that it is safe because pretty much everything can spell danger.

Being the granddaughter of survivors makes Andrea feel special, proud. She is in awe of how my father went through such terrible trauma and found a way to be a light in the darkness. It gives her hope that even the most terrible people will never succeed in breaking the human spirit.

Adina, our middle child, also describes me as being overly cautious, ever fearful that something bad might happen. She goes even further than I did, always making sure that someone knows her whereabouts. At the same time, Adina is trusting of people, a characteristic she says I passed down to her, along with a sense of confidence that everything is going to be okay, that no matter how difficult a situation may be emotionally or financially, we will get through it.

"This family legacy," Adina says, "has made me feel special in a weird kind of way. I think that's why I wanted to interview you on *StoryCorps* for Father's Day. I felt very proud when it was broadcast on NPR radio. That led to us sitting down periodically to talk more about what happened to our family during the Holocaust." Adina considers having me as her father "a victory" and "our family legacy of *menschlichkeit*, of human kindness, a gift that she shares with her children.

Adam, our youngest, agrees with his sisters that my parenting mode was risk aversive. He understands that my instinct to shield children from harm stems from what my parents went through and how they brought me up. He says, "Your dad's commitment to always try to do the right thing in the face of life-or-death circumstances has informed you as a parent and how you raised us." When Adam was on his college study-abroad program in Europe, he included a pilgrimage to Theresienstadt, the concentration camp near the Czech capital of Prague where my father was liberated.

Inherited trauma is certainly present in my children, though to a much lesser degree than how it has affected me. They have shown great empathy as I've grappled with the traumas of the Holocaust, the Yom Kippur War, and October 7, 2023. My fifth grandchild was born just a few weeks after the Hamas attack. It remains to be seen how my grandchildren will express intergenerational trauma. But this I know: Andrea, Adina, and Adam are my victory for humanity.

— *aron* —

The one constant in my life as a son of survivors is the boundless love that my parents bestowed on Rose and me. Despite all the hatred they endured, or perhaps because of it, they impressed upon us that goodness ultimately will prevail over evil. As Ma put it, "No bad person wins in the end. What did Hitler achieve?"

— *marty* —

I am in awe of my parents and of other survivors who expressed no desire for revenge against Germans or others complicit in the genocidal crimes perpetrated against them. The words of poet Iain S. Thomas come to mind: "Be soft. Do not let the world make you hard. Do not let the pain make you hate. Do not let the bitterness steal your sweetness. Take pride that even though the rest of the world may disagree, you still believe it to be a beautiful place."

Our parents mastered the art of living with trauma through their love for each other and for their children. Though Aron and I inherited the pain and sorrow they lived with, we and our children are also heirs to their qualities of love, kindness, and compassion.

acknowledgments

We are grateful to everyone who contributed to the creation of this book, beginning with our virtuoso editors, Wes Hopper and Bonny Fetterman, and copyeditors, Judy Hirt-Manheimer and Mary Beth Hinton.

Dr. Yael Danieli, thank you for sharing your encyclopedic knowledge of the subject in the foreword.

Adela Manheimer, thank you for continuing to bear witness at the age of 105 and spreading your message of love to all the good people in the world.

Rose Eichenbaum, thank you for being present at every milestone of your brother Aron's life and for being "like a sister" to Marty. Your diary proved to be an indispensable resource.

Dr. Yehoshua (Sheiky) Brownstone, thank you for adeptly rendering Yiddish words and idioms into English.

Ariel Hamu, thank you for translating your grandfather Abram Manheimer's memoir from Spanish to English.

Our life partners Judy and Marti, thank you for your steadfast support and encouragement, which fortified our resolve to bring this seven-year effort to fruition.

Our children Noah, Isaac, Mimi, Andrea, Adina, and Adam, thank you for embracing your survivor legacy with pride, love, and compassion.

Our legendary publisher Robert Mandel, thank you for your unswerving commitment to creating a body of survivor literature in response to resurgent fascism, antisemitism, and Holocaust denial.